Complexity and Innovation in Organizations

People in organizations often speak of innovation as if it were the ultimate new idea – one that would finally deliver them from the pressures of competition if they could only make the right rational choice. Since they believe that innovation is the realization of a rationally chosen goal, it is difficult to explain, even to themselves, why they never reach this promised land, and must instead keep innovating. From the perspective of rational choice, one can only conclude that failure to identify an innovation in advance is due to incompetence, and this inevitably leads to frustration and anxiety.

Complexity and Innovation in Organizations takes a different approach. Innovation is simply shown to be a new patterning of our experiences of being together, as new meaning emerges from ordinary, everyday work conversations. Viewed from a complex responsive process perspective, innovation feels less menacing and becomes a challenging, exciting process of participating with others in the evolution of work.

José Fonseca has extensive experience as a consultant in innovation and change processes for various national and international companies. He currently teaches undergraduate and postgraduate students at Universidade Lusíada in Lisbon, and the MBA programme at the Universidade Nova.

D0224712

Complexity and Emergence in Organizations

Series Editors:
Ralph D. Stacey, Douglas Griffin and Patricia Shaw
Complexity and Management Centre, University of Hertfordshire

The books in this series each give expression to a particular way of speaking about complexity in organizations. Drawing on insights from the complexity sciences, psychology and sociology, this series aims to develop theories of human organization, including ethics.

Titles in this series include:

Complexity and Management
Fad or radical challenge to systems thinking?
Ralph D. Stacey, Douglas Griffin and Patricia Shaw

Complex Responsive Processes in Organizations
Learning and knowledge creation
Ralph D. Stacey

The Paradox of Control in Organizations
Philip J. Streatfield

The Emergence of Leadership
Linking self-organization and ethics
Douglas Griffin

Complexity and Innovation in Organizations
José Fonseca

Changing the Conversation in Organizations
A complexity approach to change
Patricia Shaw

Complexity and Innovation in Organizations

José Fonseca

London and New York

First published 2002
by Routledge
2 Park Square, Milton Park, Abingdon, Oxon, OX14 4RN

Simultaneously published in the USA and Canada
by Routledge
270 Madison Ave, New York NY 10016

Routledge is an imprint of the Taylor & Francis Group

Transferred to Digital Printing 2006

Typeset in Times New Roman by Wearset Ltd, Boldon, Tyne and Wear

British Library Cataloguing in Publication Data
A catalogue record for this book is available from the British Library

Library of Congress Cataloging in Publication Data
Fonseca, José
  Complexity and innovation in organizations / José Fonseca.
    p. cm. – (Complexity and emergence in organizations)
  Includes bibliographical references and index.
    1. Technological innovations–Management. 2. Business enterprises–Technological
innovations. 3. Complex organizations–Management. I. Title. II. Series.
HD45 .F645 2001
658.5'14–dc21   2001052021

ISBN 0–415–25029–3 (hbk)
ISBN 0–415–25030–7 (pbk)

To Emília Marques – my first school teacher

What we are presently living and suffering is not just an ephemeral blistering, destined to fade away; it is, on the contrary, an epoch of transition, a bridge between what is disappearing and what will come next. And in this bridge all the currents collide, all contradictions coexist, making of it, apparently a fair of delirium, and in reality, a wonderful laboratory of life.

Bento de Jesus Caraça (1933)

Contents

Series preface   ix

1 Introduction   1
   * The paradox of innovation   4
   * The inevitability of change   5
   * Innovation as complex responsive processes of relating   7
   * Outline of the book   9

2 Mainstream thinking about innovation in organizations   11
   * Classical and neoclassical economics   11
   * Evolutionary economics   14
   * Innovation as a rational planning process   18
   * Innovation as a social and political process   21
   * The evidence   27
   * Conclusion   28

3 The role of the individual in the process of innovation   29
   * Oliveira's story of innovative concrete pipes   31
   * The role of the individual   44
   * Networks of conversations   47
   * Conclusion   49

4 The conversational nature of the innovation process   51
   * The story of systems development at a water utility   54
   * The absence of the heroic entrepreneur   66
   * Power relations   67
   * Conclusion   68

5 Innovation as complex responsive processes   69
   ⊕ The complexity sciences as source domain for analogies with
     human interaction   70
   ⊕ Interpreting the analogies in terms of human action   72
   ⊕ Differences between mainstream thinking and the perspective
     of complex responsive processes   74
   ⊕ What organizations are   75
   ⊕ How innovation arises   80
   ⊕ What innovation is   91
   ⊕ Conclusion   92

6 Innovation and the reconfiguration of power relations   94
   ⊕ The story of an electronic product catalogue   95
   ⊕ The transformation of meaning   103
   ⊕ The take off of the product catalogue   107
   ⊕ Conclusion   110

7 Conclusion   111
   ⊕ Conversation as the process of dissipating meaning   111
   ⊕ Relationship as the condition for living with anxiety   115
   ⊕ The emergence of meaning   116
   ⊕ The institutionalization of meaning   118
   ⊕ The challenge to the institutionalization of meaning   119

Bibliography   121
Index   125

Series preface
Complexity and Emergence in Organizations

The aim of this series is to give expression to a particular way of speaking about complexity in organizations, one that emphasizes the self-referential, reflexive nature of humans, the essentially responsive and participative nature of human processes of relating and the radical unpredictability of their evolution. It draws on the complexity sciences, which can be brought together with psychology and sociology in many different ways to form a whole spectrum of theories of human organization.

At one end of this spectrum there is the dominant voice in organization and management theory, which speaks in the language of design, regularity and control. In this language, managers stand outside the organizational system, which is thought of as an objective, pre-given reality that can be modeled and designed, and they control it. Managers here are concerned with the functional aspects of a system as they search for causal links that promise sophisticated tools for predicting its behaviour. The dominant voice talks about the individual as autonomous, self-contained, masterful and at the centre of an organization. Many complexity theorists talk in a language that is immediately compatible with this dominant voice. They talk about complex adaptive systems as networks of autonomous agents that behave on the basis of regularities extracted, from their environments. They talk about complex systems as objective realities that scientists can stand outside of and model. They emphasize the predictable aspects of these systems and see their modelling work as a route to increasing the ability of humans to control complex worlds.

At the other end of the spectrum there are voices from the fringes of organizational theory, complexity sciences, psychology and sociology who are defining a participative perspective. They argue that humans are themselves members of the complex networks that they form and are drawing attention to the impossibility of standing outside of them in order to objectify and model them. With this intersubjective voice people speak as subjects interacting with others in the co-evolution of a jointly constructed reality. These voices emphasize the radically unpredictable aspects of self-organizing processes and their creative potential. These are the voices of decentred agency, which talk about agents and the social world in which they live as mutually created and sustained. This way of thinking weaves together relationship psychologies and the work of complexity theorists who focus on the emergent and radically unpredictable aspects of complex systems. The result is a participative approach to understanding the complexities of organizational life.

This series is intended to give expression to the second of these voices, defining a participative perspective.

Series editors
Ralph D. Stacey, Douglas Griffin, Patricia Shaw
Complexity and Management Centre,
University of Hertfordshire

1 Introduction

- ◉ **The paradox of innovation**
- ◉ **The inevitability of change**
- ◉ **Innovation as complex responsive processes of relating**
- ◉ **Outline of the book**

Over the last few decades, innovation has become widely recognized as both a major goal of economic activity and one of the most important instruments through which organizations and countries gain and sustain competitive advantage in globally competitive marketplaces. A central plank of the European Community's industrial policy, for example, is that:

> The Community and the Member States shall ensure that the conditions necessary for the competitiveness of the Community's industry exist. For that purpose, in accordance with a system of open and competitive markets, their action shall be aimed at: ... fostering better exploitation of the industrial potential of policies of innovation, research and technological development.
>
> (European Act of 1986 – 130.1 Th.)

A close link is usually made between science and innovation as a source of competitive advantage, for example, when "Science and Technology" are identified as a cause of economic progress and a reason for the acquisition of firms in the "new" knowledge society. At the organizational level, some claim (for example, Crawford, 1991) that innovation is a key functional activity in organizations, in much the same way as marketing or finance are. Product innovation is then thought of as a routine operation like any other that organizations perform. Others suggest (for example, Eisenhardt and Tabrizi, 1995; Kanter, 1989) that innovation is a key survival strategy for organizations because it enables more rapid adaptation to turbulent environments. Innovation then becomes a primary indicator of an organization's ability to adapt to its environment (Ansoff and McDonnell, 1990). Over the past few decades, this acclamation of innovation has become highly prominent as technological and scientific advancement, particularly in information and communication, increasingly affects every aspect of people's lives.

However, when one moves away from discussing innovation at a highly abstract, macro level and turns to the literature for advice on how to be innovative in one's own organization, one finds a variety of prescriptions. These prescriptions are derived from perspectives in which innovation may be seen variously as: a characteristic of organizations called innovativeness (Quinn, 1991; Kanter, 1988; Mintzberg, 1991); an economic process of applying and spreading scientific advances (Gomory, 1989; Gibbons and Johnston, 1974); a marketing process of addressing unsatisfied needs (von Hippel, 1988); a strategic dimension of competition in high technology industries (Pavitt, 1984; de Woot, 1990; Dussage *et al.*, 1992); a routine function of organizations (Crawford, 1991); a cause of economic development through cumulative (self-reinforcing) complex interactions (Freeman, 1988); or a determinant of industrial structures and barriers to entrance (Porter, 1980).

A key question in all of these perspectives relates to how manageable the innovation process is. Those arguing that innovation is a manageable process see it as: an administrative problem (Souder, 1987; Twiss, 1992); a technical process (Wheelwright and Clark, 1992); a marketing issue (Crawford, 1991; Kotler, 1988); a social and political matter (Kanter, 1988; Frost and Egri, 1991); a cognitive and behavioural phenomenon (Van de Ven, 1988; Maidique, 1988; Howell and Higgins, 1990); or an evolutionary process (Quinn, 1991; Marquis, 1988; Gould, 1988). Furthermore, the levels at which innovation is analysed cover the range of: social systems (Lundvall, 1992); international and national economies (Freeman, 1974); industries (Abernathy and Utterback, 1988); organizations (Burns and Stalker, 1961; Quinn, 1991; Souder, 1987); groups (Kirton, 1980); and individuals (Kanter, 1984). Some claim that innovation is incremental rather than revolutionary (Quinn, 1991; Marquis, 1988). Others claim that the strategic planning of innovation is far superior to intuitive approaches (Johne and Snelson, 1990; Crawford, 1991; Cooper and Kleinschmidt, 1991). Yet others justify the superiority of soft human-centred approaches compared to strategic planning (Kanter, 1988). There are many claims of empirical validation of these perspectives. Wolfe (1994: 105) seems to be right when he says that "the most consistent theme found in the organizational innovation literature is that its research results have been inconsistent".

Despite their differences, most writers seem to accept that innovation leads to new ways of doing things and to new solutions to the problem of resource scarcity. However, even this is contested by, for example, evolutionary economists who regard innovation as more an effect than a cause of self-reinforcing, cumulative patterns of economic growth. Evolutionary economists argue that technological innovation should not be reduced to the narrow perspective of technological determinism. Others also take this position:

> The term "innovation" makes most people think first about technology . . . this is unfortunate, for our emerging world requires more social and organizational innovation. . . . Indeed, it is by now a virtual truism that if technical innovation runs far ahead of complementary social and organizational innovation, its use in practice can be either dysfunctional or negligible.
>
> (Kanter, 1984: 20)

Regardless of whether innovation is thought of as a "hard" scientific and technological process, a rational management process, or a "soft" intuitive human process, all these perspectives have in common the assumption that innovation is a phenomenon that can be subjected to human control. It is taken for granted that humans can purposefully design, in advance, the conditions under which innovation will occur. In this book, I will argue that this assumption of controllability is the distinguishing feature of what I will call mainstream thinking about innovation. In my view, mainstream thinking is basically systems thinking. The purpose of this book is to argue for a very different understanding of innovation, one drawing on the perspectives developed in some detail in earlier volumes of the series of which this book is part (Stacey, 2001; Stacey et al., 2000). Innovation will be presented as the emergent continuity and transformation of patterns of human interaction, understood as ongoing, ordinary complex responsive processes of human relating in local situations in the living present. It is in such patterns of interaction that innovative meanings emerge, often to be expressed in the reified symbols of books, procedural manuals and computer programs, for example, and in material artefacts such as communication equipment. Mainstream thinking about innovation tends to downplay the messy relational processes in which reifications and artefacts have emerged to become tools in the ongoing interactive processes of organizing and earning a living. Instead, mainstream thinking tends to focus attention on the emergent reifications and tools as if they were innovation itself. In this book I will be focusing attention on the ongoing self-organizing processes of communicative interaction in which the products of innovation emerge, and I will be arguing that these are not controllable. I will be drawing on actual experiences of innovation in order to develop my argument. These experiences are not idealizations of the innovation process that recount huge success stories in the world's largest organizations in the world's most advanced economy. Instead, they are accounts of the ordinary everyday processes in which organizations evolve, at a particular time, in a particular country, namely, Portugal.

But, first consider the kind of problem that mainstream ways of thinking about innovation lead to.

The paradox of innovation

Organizations create novelty in the form of better, more reliable, attractive and useful products and services. As consumers, we have become addicted to this spiral of novelty, demanding more and more from organizations. However, those organizations seem to be the first victims of their creations. Each individual organization struggles to get ahead of the competition in order to enjoy, even if only for a short time, some security and market protection. In doing so, they jointly create immense instability. Nowadays, facing the world as their market, and so even more competitive threats and demanding consumers, organizations seem to have no alternative but to keep innovating. As they struggle to achieve some stability, so they keep creating more and more complexity. This, it seems to me, is the paradox of innovation: the activity of innovating so as to create security and stability is that which produces insecurity and instability. There is, however, no escape from this paradox in the modern world. Individually, organizations adopt extraordinarily complicated and sometimes senseless procedures to predict and control their futures. They strive to keep up with whatever prospects they envision. Ironically, however, the more they act in order to secure their future, the more the compound outcome of their individual behaviours results in complex interrelations that render the future even more unpredictable and surprising.

People in organizations often talk about innovation as if there was some ultimate novelty, one that would finally deliver them from the pressures of competition, if only they could make the right rational choice. But as they all do this, they become trapped in the paradox described above, to which there is no resolution. And since they believe that innovation is the realization of a rationally chosen goal, it is difficult for them to explain, even to themselves, why they never reach the "Promised Land" but must keep innovating. From the perspective of rational choice, one can only conclude that failure to identify an innovation in advance is due to incompetence and this inevitably leads to frustration and anxiety. However, the range of feelings is quite different if one thinks of innovation as new meaning emerging in ordinary, everyday work conversations holding the potential for the construction of reifications and material artefacts. Innovation is then simply new patterning of our experience of being together. From a complex responsive process perspective, innovation feels less menacing and becomes a challenging, exciting process of participating with others in the evolution of work.

Imagine what would have happened if, before setting off to India to establish the first sea route between West and East in the fifteenth century, the Portuguese navigator, Vasco da Gama, had been required to fill in the paperwork that the European Union now demands before it will fund a new venture. Portuguese children today would not be fascinated by stories of sea monsters, mermaids, storms, famine, suffering, perseverance and courage. Instead, they would be puzzled by epic narratives about milestones, deliverables, accounting procedures, reports, review meetings, market plans, and detailed discounted cashflow analyses. One of the consequences of mainstream thinking is the loss of a sense of the excitement of creating the truly new. This is replaced by the belief that movement into the future is simply the uncovering of hidden order, the realization of some chosen goal, the unfolding of some stable form already enfolded, or the intentional production of the variety required to match uncertain conditions.

The inevitability of change

We are repeatedly told that we live in a world of accelerating change and the word "globalization" seems to capture both the menace and the promise of this change. We are frequently exhorted to jump onto the high-speed train of change if we want to avoid extinction. However, there is nothing new about change: there has been change since the beginning of the universe. Globalization began as soon as the first humans wandered across the continents and later, Roman roads, Portuguese and Spanish sailing ventures, industrial revolutions and many other economic and technological developments were quantum leaps in globalization. Innovation and globalization have always been features of life.

However, while there is always change, periods of change differ from one another. Unlike previous economic revolutions, in which the input was energy and matter (coal, steam, oil, electricity, steel, plastic), the present revolution in economic productivity is based on information and knowledge (Freeman, 1988). This is a monumental shift. Previous changes could be adequately understood in terms of linear relations between material realities, enabling us to hold onto what may be the "illusion of control". The new dimensions of change can only be understood in nonlinear terms (Arthur, 1996). We have moved from an economy based on the transformation of energy and matter to an economy of knowledge creation. Thus, we have moved from one reality of designing machinery, for which the natural sciences could supply the tools of measurement and calculation, to a more subjective reality, where the old notions of measurement and calculation do not apply (Caraça, 1993). Many do not really believe this and so engage in extraordinary efforts to develop "frameworks" for measuring, and thus controlling, relationships, knowledge and conversations.

Innovation is part of humankind's struggle for identity and survival. The human race has faced the problem of resource scarcity and other natural constraints and has, so far successfully, dealt with this situation by creating new solutions, some of which also turn out to be harmful. And we have been able to do this in relating with others in dynamic processes of communicative interaction in which new patterns of meaning (action) have been constantly arising. Perhaps now, however, we have passed a critical point and entered a more intense sphere of interrelating. Perhaps we have been developing greater diversity and greater complexity and this has led us to be less dependent on our natural environment and its material and energy constraints. If this is so, then our sense-making requires a much more human-centred approach, one that focuses attention on our experience of being together, than that to be found in mainstream thinking about innovation. This book explores innovation from such a perspective, in which innovation is understood to emerge in complex responsive processes of relating.

Innovation as complex responsive processes of relating

The complex responsive process (Stacey, 2001; Stacey *et al.*, 2000) view of organizational life understands organizations to be patterns of relationship between people:

> All human relationships, including the communicative action of a body with itself, that is mind, and the communicative actions between bodies, that is the social, are interweaving story lines and propositions constructed by those relationships at the same time as those story lines and propositions construct the relationships. They are all complex responsive processes of relating that can be thought of as the interweaving of themes, and variations on those themes, that recursively form themselves.
>
> (Stacey, 2001: 140)

These processes of communicative interaction are self-organizing and their patterning changes in unpredictable ways. But at the same time, the constraints of power and ideology, and the dynamics of inclusion–exclusion, emerge in communicative interaction, providing coherence and control although no one is in control. It is the very features of the process of interaction, namely, taking turns, using rhetorical devices, categorizing, and so on, in the context of mutual expectations, that imparts coherence and pattern to people's ongoing communicative interactions.

From this perspective, organizations are thought of as groups of biological individuals relating to each other in the medium of symbols, thereby forming, while simultaneously being formed by, figurations of power relations between them, and between their group or organization and others in a community. The ongoing processes of relating always have a history: the history of each individual and of the group, organization, community and wider society, all of which are processes of relating. The processes of relating also encompass a particular physical place, particular resource availabilities and particular tools and technologies.

To put it in another way, organizational life is social practice, that is, patterns in the ongoing dealings of individuals with each other, sustained through time and across space in the medium of the very practices themselves. These practices are both the outcome and the medium of individual interactions in the process of which individual capacities for action are themselves formed. Human subjects and social institutions are jointly constituted through recurrent practices.

From this perspective knowledge is meaning and it can only emerge in the communicative interaction between people. It emerges as meaning in the ongoing relating between people in the living present. This is an evolutionary concept of knowledge as meaning continuously reproduced and potentially transformed in action. Knowledge is, therefore, the thematic patterns organizing the experience of being together. The process of learning is much the same and there does not seem to be much point in trying to distinguish the one from the other. Identity, both individual and collective, evolves and communicative interaction, learning and knowledge creation are essentially the same processes as the evolution of identity. It is meaningless to ask whether organizations learn or whether people in organizations learn. It is the same process. It is meaningless to ask how tacit knowledge is transformed into explicit knowledge, since unconscious and conscious themes organizing experience are inseparable facets of the same process. Organizational change, learning and knowledge creation are the same as change in communicative interaction, whether people are conscious of it or not. This perspective suggests that the conversational life of people in an organization is of primary importance.

This view of complex responsive processes is the point of departure for a way of understanding innovation and knowledge creation that I will be exploring in this book. I will argue that innovation is the emergence of new meaning and that such new meaning emerges in conversations between people that are characterized by a paradoxical dynamic of understanding and misunderstanding at the same time. One strand of the complexity sciences is the theory of dissipative structures (Prigogine and Stengers, 1984). A dissipative structure is a natural phenomenon that is continuously sustained by the process of dispersing energy or information. It is the process of dissipating, even wasting, energy that imparts changeability to the phenomenon and it is in the unstable, even chaotic, dynamics at bifurcation (change) points that the phenomenon is transformed. In other words, new order emerges in disorder, that is, diversity and what seems like wasteful interaction. Drawing on analogies from dissipative structure theory, I will be suggesting that innovation in organizations is fundamentally a conversational process in which meaning is continuously dispersed. Innovation as the potential for transformation emerges in conversations between people that are characterized by redundant diversity, which is experienced as mis/understanding. By this I mean that conversations having the potential for transformed meaning do not simply reproduce knowledge already formed, so sustaining identity, but rather dissipate meaning, leading to the transformation of identity. In speaking of the dissipation of meaning, I am referring to the misunderstanding in the midst of understanding that provokes people into searching for new ways of being together in the living present. It is in the communicative interaction of such searching that new meaning might emerge.

I will argue that these processes of probing interaction generate anxiety as identities are questioned, consciously and unconsciously. The emergence of trust is required to sustain the anxiety-provoking conversations, characterized by redundant diversity experienced as misunderstanding, which are required for innovation to emerge. I will argue that these processes of dissipation are fundamentally uncertain, making it impossible to design in advance the settings that will produce innovations. I will argue that innovation, new meaning, is prior to the "phases" generally identified in models of innovation "management" and that these phase models start at the stage where innovation has already emerged. What these models are able to supply, therefore, is a set of tools, that is, reified knowledge that people participating in the processes of innovation might find useful in the communicative process, but which cannot bring the order and predictability they claim.

Outline of the book

Chapter 2 distinguishes between two major strands in mainstream thinking about innovation in organizations. In the first strand, innovation is understood as a rational planning process; the origins of this kind of thinking can be traced back to classical and neoclassical economics. The second strand has its origins in what has come to be known as evolutionary economics and it understands innovation as an entrepreneurial and social process, where social means political interaction conditioned by culture. This strand contests the rational planning view and holds that innovation arises in the intuitive, visionary actions of entrepreneurs operating within supportive cultures. These two strands of thinking both hold that innovation originates as intention in the mind of the autonomous individual and that it is either directly manageable and controllable or indirectly manageable through the assumed ability to design the social conditions in which innovation will emerge. Both strands produce empirical evidence to support their different perspectives, often using the same case studies but making very different interpretations of how the innovation occurred.

Chapter 3 presents the story of an individual entrepreneur who developed the innovative design and manufacture of concrete drainpipes. The chapter will be pointing to how the innovation cannot be understood purely in terms of this individual entrepreneur, even though he was extremely important. Instead, the story reveals how the innovation emerged in networks of conversations between people from diverse backgrounds. This is a story of constant shifts in meaning as people struggled to understand each other.

Another story of innovation is provided in Chapter 4. This time there was no individual entrepreneur who can plausibly be said to have been the originator of the innovation, namely, a digitized survey of drainpipes in the streets of Lisbon. The conversational nature of the innovation process becomes even clearer in this story of many transformations in the meaning of the innovation. It also becomes clear how transformations of meaning are intertwined with shifting patterns of power relations.

In Chapter 5, I present a brief review of the theory of complex responsive processes of relating and indicate how, from this perspective, one might make sense of the innovation process recounted in the previous chapters. I will be developing the analogy between dissipative structure theory and the conversational process having the potential for transformation.

Chapter 6 provides another narrative of innovation, this time, the story of how an electronic product catalogue was developed. What I particularly want to point to in this chapter is the reconfiguring of power relations that is always involved in the innovation process.

Finally, in Chapter 7, I present some general conclusions and implications of understanding innovation as a conversational process in which meaning is dissipated.

2 Mainstream thinking about innovation in organizations

⊛ **Classical and neoclassical economics**
⊛ **Evolutionary economics**
⊛ **Innovation as a rational planning process**
⊛ **Innovation as a social and political process**
⊛ **The evidence**
⊛ **Conclusion**

The word "innovation" conjures up many different meanings in fields of inquiry as diverse as economics, management, organizational behaviour, sociology, engineering, biology, psychology, history and political science. The origins of current mainstream management thinking about innovation in organizations are to be found in economic theory and in this chapter I explore those origins and how they have influenced current thinking. The chapter first considers how innovation is dealt with in classical and neoclassical economics, and how this led to one of the main strands of current thinking about innovation, namely, the view of innovation as a rational, planned process. The chapter then goes on to look at some key features of what has come to be called evolutionary economics and how this is expressed in views of innovation as an entrepreneurial and social process, the other main strand of current thinking. This provides the context within which the different view I propose in this book might be understood.

Classical and neoclassical economics

Classical economic theory does not deal with the dynamics of growth, but rather with the functioning of markets as resource allocation mechanisms in which demand functions interact with supply functions to determine prices that balance supply and demand, so sustaining market equilibrium. Just as with classical physics, an economy is understood to move according to deterministic laws in which the future is a predictable repetition of the past and the question of innovation does not feature, other than as an unexplained shift in the supply function. Movement into the future proceeds in a regular manner according to the equivalent of natural laws. The purpose of the movement is to sustain a predictable state of equilibrium specified by the economic laws of supply and demand, the equivalent of natural laws. When one talks about the nature and purpose of the movement of some phenomenon one is talking about teleology as the cause of the movement. The first volume (Stacey *et al.*, 2000) of the series in which this book appears referred to movement that is the repetition of the past with the "purpose" of sustaining equilibrium as "Natural Law Teleology". Classical economic thinking about market systems thus assumes Natural Law Teleology. Within market systems, classical economic theory conceived of people in a particular way, namely, as rational individuals. These rational individuals (economic man) were thought of as operating in a calculating way in markets driven by the laws of supply and demand. Each rational individual calculated the predicted economic consequences of every action as determined by the laws of the market, choosing those actions that maximized their individual utilities. Individuals were assumed to act as profit and utility maximizers and, because they behaved in this way, markets functioned efficiently to optimize resource allocation. Stacey *et al.* (2000) refer to this way of thinking as "Rationalist Teleology". This is a way of thinking about movement as being caused by the rational choices of autonomous individuals in order to achieve their chosen goals. The point, then, is that classical economic theorizing is conducted within dual causal frameworks of Natural Law Teleology at the macro level of market clearing and Rationalist Teleology at the micro level of individual economic agency. In the former there is no choice or freedom and in the latter choice is reduced to a rational calculation. Both of these ways of thinking are incompatible with the notion of novelty or innovation.

In the neoclassical development of economic theory, which continued within the dual causal framework described above, innovation was incorporated as a variable in the supply/production function. Independent variables, or mechanisms, were identified as causes of innovation and it was then a short step to assume that managers, as rational calculating agents, could operate on at least some of these independent variables and so exercise control over innovation. Innovation, then, was equated with independent technological and, less frequently, organizational changes, which were thought of as changing the position and shape of production functions, usually by replacing the labour factor of production with capital. Changes, intentional or otherwise, in the independent causes of innovation had the effect of altering production functions. Consequent output and cost changes disturbed market equilibrium and market forces immediately came into play to produce a new equilibrium state. How the technological and organizational innovations came about in the first place were not explained in neoclassical economic theory, but simply taken as given causes embodied in capital assets or in the knowledge required to manage capital and labour resources. This way of thinking led to a search for the specific variables and circumstances that would cause innovation to occur and enable managers to control it.

Although Solow (1957) empirically identified the variable "technical progress" as a major explanation of growth, understood as shifts in production functions, it proved difficult to specify appropriate independent causal variables to explain "technical progress". Consequently, the cause of "technical progress" had to be represented as a "residual" in the mathematical models of economic growth; empirical studies showed that these residual variables accounted for 60 per cent of the growth and that 80 per cent of the growth attributed to labour productivity was due to technical development (Denison, 1962). In other words, the models simply showed that innovation was important and that it could not be explained. All that could be said was that innovations appeared and disturbed market equilibria, which were then restored by the operation of the laws of the market. However, it might take a long time for equilibrium to be restored and this could open up the possibility of temporary monopolies, so that innovation becomes a source of monopolistic power and more than "normal" profit. The rational assessment of potential monopoly profits then becomes the prime motivator of innovation activity.

The neoclassical understanding of innovation, therefore, represents a "both ... and" way of thinking. At one level, that of whole economies and markets, innovation is understood as a variable in the economic laws, a form of Natural Law Teleology, which produces efficient outcomes and sustains equilibrium states. At another level, that of the industry, innovation is understood as a choice that organizations make on rational grounds in order to secure temporary monopoly positions and so maximize their profit goals. This is Rationalist Teleology, which is also applied at the level of the individual manager. It is autonomous rational individuals who select innovations on the basis of rational predictions and calculations in order to maximize their organization's profits. Two different ways of thinking are thus employed, sometimes one and sometimes the other, depending upon the level of analysis. In one way of thinking innovation is understood as a variable in a deterministic market system driven by the equivalent of natural laws; in the other way of thinking it is thought of as a variable, the consequences of which rational managers can predict and hence choose to control. In this "both . . . and" thinking any sense of the paradox of determinism and choice is simply eliminated.

Evolutionary economics

A very different way of thinking about innovation is to be found in what has come to be called evolutionary economics, most notably in the work of Schumpeter (1934). He was interested in explaining why economic growth occurs, rather than simply ascribing it to an unexplained residual; his main contribution was to place innovation inside the economic system rather than considering it as an exogenous shock to which economic systems reacted. He argued that an economy could not be understood as an entity independent of society as a whole and that economic growth had to be explained in terms of the dynamics of scientific and technological innovation and the roles of entrepreneurs in organizations. For him, innovation was to be understood in terms of *both* social/organizational dynamics *and* individual psychology. Schumpeter distinguished between the entrepreneur who performed a role, and innovation, which was the outcome of entrepreneurial activity in organizations that possessed characteristics making it possible for individuals to take the role of entrepreneur. For him, the "entrepreneur" played a central role in the process of economic development. Several people could take this role and none would play it all the time. He therefore thought about economic growth in terms of dynamic processes, rather than in terms of the mechanisms that featured in neoclassical economics. Furthermore, Schumpeter addressed the issue of innovation within a systemic framework. An innovation could thus be a new output that the organization placed in its environment, a new input it received from the environment, or a new way of arranging its internal relations, including the psychological attributes of individuals.

Schumpeter was also the first to address the issue of knowledge creation, knowledge transfer and knowledge use, as underlying the process of innovation. In fact this is a central tenet of his views, making of the process of knowledge creation, particularly when embodied into some technological artefact, an endogenous phenomenon of economic realities. Even though he understood innovation as a linear path from basic science to a commercial application of scientific knowledge, he did not restrict innovation to purely scientific ventures. His definition of innovation comprised all ways of doing things differently.

Schumpeter's view of economic activity differs from that of neoclassical economics at a fundamental level to do with the nature of movement into the future and the purpose of such movement. As mentioned above, neoclassical economics is a way of thinking in terms of *both* Natural Law Teleology, in which innovation is ascribed to unexplained external shocks, which are adjusted to according to the laws of the market, *and* Rationalist Teleology, in which rationally calculating individuals choose how to operate on, or respond to, the external shocks. Schumpeter took a position based on Darwinian evolutionary theory and argued that the movement of an economy into the future was unpredictable because innovation made the future different from the past rather than just a repetition. For him, the dynamic of economic growth was not a move to equilibrium but a continuous disequilibrating process. Chance innovations continually disturbed equilibrium states requiring organizations and individuals to adapt in the present in order to survive.

Stacey *et al.* (2000) have called this way of thinking Adaptionist Teleology. Movement here is toward an unknowable future driven by chance variation and competitive selection, in order to survive. As I have already said, Schumpeter also understood innovation in systemic terms when he talked about organizations having characteristics that made it possible for individuals to take up entrepreneurial roles. This implies that innovation is the unfolding of patterns of behaviour already enfolded in particular organizational dynamics. In the classification of ways of thinking about causality suggested by Stacey *et al.* (2000), this unfolding of enfolded pattern is typical of systems thinking and they have called it Formative Teleology. Here, movement of the phenomenon is the unfolding of what is already enfolded in it in order to realize a mature state of itself. A shift from neoclassical economics to evolutionary economics as a way of thinking about innovation therefore amounts to a shift from thinking about causality in terms of Natural Law Teleology to a way of thinking in terms of Adaptionist and/or Formative Teleology. In the former novelty and freedom are pure chance and in the latter there is neither novelty nor freedom. However, in his emphasis on the autonomous individual as entrepreneur, Schumpeter retained a place for thinking in terms of Rationalist Teleology. In other words, innovation was also caused by the choices autonomous individuals made about the goals of innovations and the actions required to bring them into being. He did not think about the autonomous individual as a rational calculator but rather as an intuitive, visionary entrepreneur. Schumpeter's thought, therefore, retains a dual theory of causality, namely, both Adaptionist/Formative Teleology of the macro system and the Rationalist Teleology of the individual innovator at the micro level. Once again there is the elimination of paradox, this time the paradox of innovation arising in the operation of competitive selection on chance changes, or innovation as the unfolding of enfolded conditions, and also the purposeful, deliberate choices of individuals. In the end, the origin of novelty lies in individual heads.

In the rest of this chapter, I want to explore how the two very different ways of dealing with the question of innovation, represented by neoclassical economics, on the one hand, and evolutionary economics, on the other, have been taken up in the literature on organizations and their management.

Much of the discussion about innovation in the management and organizational literature is conducted from the macro perspective of markets and economies. For example, there has been a continuing debate about the relative importance of the market in triggering innovation, on the one hand, and technological development as the origin of innovation, on the other. The very posing of the question reflects the way in which neoclassical economics distinguishes between demand and supply functions. The question is whether growth occurs primarily because of changes on the demand side or changes on the supply side. Those focusing attention on the market and demand pull tend not to perceive the organizations as the producer of innovation but, rather, the adopter of an innovation. A key issue from this perspective is how an innovation, required as a response to environmental change, is either accepted or rejected, and this leads to the interest in patterns of innovation diffusion among populations of adopters (Rogers, 1983) and prescriptions for fine tuning the positioning variables of an organization's marketing strategy. The aim is to position a company's marketing mix (Kotler, 1988) so that it "fits" the marketplace in an optimal way.

Another key question has to do with how one organization assimilates and implements an innovation and what makes it more or less prone to do so. This leads to attempts to identify the determinants of behaviour in innovative organizations and how they differ from those that are not innovative. Those emphasizing the supply side explore the making of an innovation in terms of new product and technological development. Here, innovation is not thought of as the action of adopting some finished, finite and well-defined novelty but, rather, as the action of developing novelty. The orientation here is from the organization outwards as opposed to the inward orientation of those who emphasize the external origins of innovation in organizations.

It is not relevant, for the purposes of this book, to explore any further the issues raised by the macro level analyses of innovation. What is relevant is an understanding of how neoclassical and evolutionary economic theories have formed the foundations of thinking about how innovation does, or should, take place in organizations. As we will see, the primary concern of writers about innovation in organizations is with how organizations should innovate, rather than how they actually do so.

Thinking about the process of innovation in mainstream literature on the subject seems to me to fall into two streams. First, some think of innovation as a rational, intentional, sequential managerial process. Thinking here reflects the rational behaviour assumption of classical and neoclassical economics and falls within the paradigm of strategic choice and planning. Firms innovate in direct, purposeful and intentional responses to objective changes in their environment, so that they can achieve a new equilibrium. The future competitive positioning is a matter of forecasting and of detecting shifts in consumer preferences or in detecting latent unsatisfied demands. Acquiring this information involves an effort that is similar to the application of the scientific method. Second, there are those who understand innovation to be a social, political and behavioural process, reflecting the position of evolutionary economics. This stream, while rejecting the rational paradigm and embracing a human-centred view, does not reject the importance of equilibrium. It only denies the ability of rational ways of achieving it. As an alternative, it proposes shared visions and culture as organizational binders and control devices to attain desired behaviours. This section now reviews each of these streams of thinking and how they display the influence of neoclassical and evolutionary economics.

Innovation as a rational planning process

In accordance with the Rationalist Teleological framework of thought to be found in both neoclassical and evolutionary economics, innovation is seen as a prime strategic goal of organizations to be realized through particular organizational functions. For example, the influential writings of Drucker (1985) suggest that innovation is the function of entrepreneurship, and that this function is an essential characteristic for survival, not only of small or new businesses, but also of large, already existing organizations. For Drucker, the conduct of innovative activities and the creation of new products is the result of a conscious and purposeful search. He ascribes successful innovation to the systematic search for opportunities and latent consumer needs. The routinization of the activity of innovation is taken even further by writers such as Crawford (1991) and Souder (1987). They also argue that innovation is essential for survival in a fast changing environment and that this requires organizations to establish distinct departments to take responsibility for the coordination and execution of the tasks required to renew a company's products. For these authors the development of new products seems to be mainly that of managing product life cycles through monitoring the market, assessing consumer responses to existing products, and replacing losers with new improved products that will fit market demand. Innovation is subservient to company goals and strategic aims, which guide the search for new opportunities.

Many of those who think of innovation as an administrative or managerial problem in this way tend to build formal models of the process. For example, Cooper (1990) studied and promoted NASA's Phased Project Planning. This is a sequential procedure consisting of discrete tasks; at the end of each task there is a revision procedure called a "decision gate". The procedure prescribes a halt on tasks until previous ones are accomplished as a precondition for further budget approvals and the release of funds to finance subsequent phases. The sequence is as follows:

- Initial Idea, which must be screened and evaluated through Gate 1.
- If the idea is approved it enters Stage 1, where the technical and market conditions necessary for success are assessed. If these preconditions are satisfied, then there is a perceived market for a feasible idea and there is a move to Stage 2.
- Stage 2 consists of the elaboration of a product concept. This product concept is judged against competing concepts on Gate 3 and if it is approved it becomes a business decision to develop that concept.

- Stage 3 consists of the development of the concept into material reality. Gate 4 revises the outcome of the effort so far.
- Stage 5 sets a battery of technical tests and validation of the trials performed. Gate 5 assesses the commercial potential of the product.
- Stage 6 consists of the launching of the product. This is normally associated with programming tools such as PERT/CPM developed by the US Navy and by Dupont de Nemours (Koontz *et al.*, 1984) to manage numerous suppliers, coordinating the timing of deliveries and the performance of tasks.

Crawford (1991) presents a model that is similar to Cooper's. It too is an algorithm for systematically screening ideas and monitoring customers, top managers, employees, unused resources and competitors, all regarded as sources of innovation. The screening produces an inventory of potential new concepts, which are subjected to strategic appraisal in which they must be justified in two ways. First, they must contribute to the realization of the strategy and, second, they must match some customer need, which has been identified in advance. That is to say, promoting some novel idea implies possessing a clear product concept (technical/economic feasibility) before actually creating it, which might then be rejected because it does not fit with the strategy. Crawford's recommendations for the idea screening of stage one are as follows. If the new concepts pass the hurdles, then they are evaluated against competing strategic ideas. This is done by factor value analysis, under which a product might be "decomposed" into some 200 (or more) descriptive items. The result of this phase is a new concept, which is formally accepted for the development stages, although the concept continues to be revised and analysed in detail. Then the new product concept moves into further market, engineering and financial analysis. This consists of further refinement of previous steps. If the market is clearly identified, if there are no remaining engineering difficulties, and if a projected cashflow meets the organizational standards, then planning of the realization of the concept begins. This phase includes: securing resources, establishing the development team, distributing responsibilities, scheduling tasks such as prototype development, consumer tests, review meetings, and so on. All of these matters are supposed to be arranged and designed in advance and incorporated in the business plan.

Defining sequential models of the innovation process in this way quite clearly displays systems thinking. Those who think in this way are describing and prescribing cybernetic systems for use in the control of the innovation process, which is understood as a rational planning activity. In taking this view they are thinking within the framework of Formative Teleology, in that the system is the formative cause of the process of innovation. However, the inherent difficulty in thinking in this way is that it precludes genuine novelty, the very phenomenon one is trying to understand. This is because when innovation proceeds according to a system it must be unfolding what is already enfolded as the design of the system. In moving from the macro level of markets to the micro level of intra-organizational behaviour, therefore, writers taking the approach outlined here are substituting the causal framework of Formative Teleology for that of Natural Law Teleology found in neoclassical economics, while retaining a place for the Rationalist Teleology of the autonomous individual. They therefore end up with a framework in which innovation is understood both in terms of Formative Teleology and in terms of Rationalist Teleology in a way that eliminates any paradox. To repeat, the paradox arises by proposing that autonomous individuals choose the innovation, in effect putting an intention into the system, but are also parts of the system, which unfolds what has been put into it: an individual is said to be free to choose but is also subject to the operation of the system. This paradox is not addressed, but eliminated, in the "both ... and" way of thinking in which there is *both* the Formative Teleology of a system *and* the Rationalist Teleology of the autonomous individual. Furthermore, neither Rationalist nor Formative Teleology really explains how innovations originate in the first place. The former simply regards them as the deliberate choices of autonomous individuals, without explaining how they make those choices other than ascribing them to rationality. The latter regards the innovation as the unfolding of a design, again without explaining how the design enfolds innovations.

To summarize, the key features of the rational planning approach to innovation are the ways in which the origins of innovation are located in the reasoning capacity of the autonomous individual, who takes the position of the objective observer and chooses the goals for a mechanistic system of a cybernetic kind, which then unfolds the innovation enfolded in its design. Now consider the very different approach taken by those who subscribe to evolutionary economics.

Innovation as a social and political process

A number of writers have pointed to the limitations of thinking about the innovation process as one of rational design and they argue for a perspective that harks back to Schumpeter's work. For example, population ecology theorists (Hannan and Freeman, 1977) claim that rules of competition are not set by an individual organization but are established in the adaptive interaction between organizations within the wider population of organizations. New entrepreneurial businesses may build up a configuration of resources and competencies, and competitive selection will soon sort out the most successful from the others. Leading organizations emerge, to be mimicked by others. However, complacency and inertia soon establish a trajectory that constrains individual organizations, making it extremely difficult for them to change. As industries continue to evolve with the appearance of new entrepreneurial organizations, the older ones are weeded out by competitive selection. From this evolutionary perspective, it is whole populations of organizations that change through competitive selection applied to both emerging new individual organizations and to old ones that have become stuck and eventually suffer extinction. This is very much in line with Schumpeter's "gales of creative destruction" and it reflects the Adaptionist Teleological framework of his way of thinking. However, this perspective has not become part of mainstream thinking about innovation, probably because of the very limited role it gives to managerial choice. Strategic choice theory argues that individual organizations may get stuck in states of inertia but that they do have the capacity to choose changes. For them, change takes place at the level of the organization and it is these changes that change the population of organizations.

However, although Schumpeter's (1939) work has not entered mainstream thinking in a straightforward way, it has nevertheless had a significant impact. A number of writers have picked up on his suggestion that innovation starts with the creation of scientific knowledge. They have argued that advancements in science, translated by technological institutions into technical, instrumental knowledge, are passed on to organizations possessing the Research and Development (R&D) resources required to translate such new knowledge into products, and marketing departments to position those products in the market. Organizations, therefore, are conceived of as the agents of innovation: institutions that mediate the transformation of scientific knowledge into concrete material realities with wide social use (Nelson and Winter, 1982). Here, the focus shifts from the single variable explanations of neoclassical economics, explored in terms of econometric identification of correlations between R&D expenditure and economic performance, to more idiosyncratic agency models. These models take account of how cultural variables, biased decision-making strategies and managerial procedures mediate processes of transferring, adding value to and utilizing the new knowledge flowing between the institutions of science and industrial companies. Writers in this tradition draw on Schein's (1988) theory of leadership and corporate culture. This theory understands culture to be a system of beliefs supported by basic assumptions of which people are not aware. Culture understood in this way is a system of emotional affiliation between people that produces behavioural conformity. Schein argued that it was the prime function of leadership to identify and manage the cultural system of an organization in the interests of securing desired organizational behaviour; this could include the behaviour required for innovation. Peters and Waterman (1982) were other important proponents of this view, with their emphasis on values and visionary leadership. Schumpeter's thinking has been incorporated into this kind of thinking about cultural systems and the role of charismatic, visionary leaders; in so doing it represents a shift from the framework of Adaptionist Teleology to one of Formative Teleology, the way of thinking about causality that underlies all systems thinking. This cultural system, which it is the responsibility of leaders to design in terms of values and visions, enfolds the behavioural conditions and the purpose required for the unfolding of innovation.

Politics and culture

An influential example of this line of thinking is provided by the work of Kanter (1984, 1988). She rejects a planned approach to innovation because innovation entails too much uncertainty and ambiguity as to the nature of opportunities, goals, costs and timings to make planning possible. There is usually more than one solution to any technical difficulty and the knowledge created in innovations is at first mainly tacit and so cannot be easily communicated. Added to this, innovations tend to cross an organization's functional boundaries, threatening the interests of established groups and so generating conflict. The innovation process is, therefore, essentially one of political negotiation. Frost and Egri (1991: 231) take much the same position:

Innovation at its core is about ambiguity and is replete with disputes caused by differences in perspectives among those touched by an innovation and the change it engenders, we believe that innovation often becomes a very political process.

Those whose interests are threatened by innovation will seek to counter innovative ideas and so damp creativity, unless there is a culture that fosters innovation and unless those in senior hierarchical positions act as champions of innovation, protecting innovators, lobbying on their behalf and supplying the resources they require. What Kanter proposes is the substitution of rational rules and goals by an affiliative social system based on trust or faith as processes for controlling behaviour and performance. Rationally designed planning systems are replaced by systems based on shared culture and the visions of charismatic leaders. She is concerned with the impact on productivity if people ignore social and behavioural variables in the introduction or in the creation of a technical innovation; as an alternative to the plan, she proposes culture and visionary leaders as a system that binds people together. If leaders establish favourable conditions, then people can be relied upon to practice self-control and act in the best interests of the organization in the knowledge that those who do not act in accordance with the organizational credo will encounter peer pressure and will have to leave the organization if they do not comply.

Kanter is, therefore, arguing that social arrangements foster innovation and that an organization's leaders can design these social arrangements into a organization. The key feature of these social arrangements is flexible managerial practices that allow individual creativity to emerge. She prescribes empowerment, that is, a form of leadership that allows people to take risks. She exhorts leaders to foster entrepreneurship through installing: a culture of risk taking and a systematic focus on serving the customer; reward systems that motivate innovators; and financial slack that allows them to experiment. Kanter claims that there is empirical validation of the positive connection between innovation and the social arrangements she suggests. The keys to supportive social arrangements and effective political processes are visionary leadership and entrepreneurial individuals. The design of social, cultural and political systems required for innovation is the responsibility of the leaders, who must establish the "right" environment for people to develop their creative potential. That "right" environment offers incentives and protection for entrepreneurial individuals who go against the prevailing order. The establishment of these conditions, she suggests, will allow leaders to rely on the self-organized realization of the innovation process.

She repeatedly emphasizes the importance for innovation of exceptional individuals. Kanter's entrepreneur is a special character, typically possessing transformational leadership traits: a hero who fights the bureaucracy and the status quo. Product champions subvert procedures and use influence tactics to gain attention and resources to materialize their visions (Howell and Higgins, 1990). Other writers also take this view of the special status of the entrepreneurial individual, classifying people into innovators and adapters. These categories are then used as predictors of team performance: superior teams have a balanced composition of innovators and adaptors (Kirton, 1980). Functioning teams are also central in Kanter's view of the innovation process and this leads to concern with the politics of cross-functional working (Kanter, 1988). Recognizing that parochial attitudes and interests often drive groups, Kanter suggested the design of cross-functional teams, which would be more effective when the promoter of innovation invited people to participate. Henderson and Clark (1990) suggested that nowadays innovations take the form of what they called "architectural innovations", by which they meant the fusion of several technologies, for example, the melding of information and communication technologies that gave birth to the Internet. Connection then requires the setting up of dialogues between different technical languages. The issue becomes one of integrating the core competencies of organizations (Hamel and Prahalad, 1989).

Kanter also suggests that there are phases for the innovation process that differ significantly from the rational phases discussed in the previous section. For her, the innovation process moves through the phases of: idea generation, requiring people to step outside their usual contexts; coalition building, in which people negotiate support and access to resources for a new idea; idea realization, which requires sustaining the expectations of those backing the new idea; and innovation diffusion. For Kanter innovation is a primary purpose of an organization. She seems to dismiss rationalism altogether because it focuses on stability and on avoiding surprises. Therefore, it misses the potential for creativity. She posits the creation of instability as endless cycles of novelty, showing little concern for efficiency, which is at the centre of concern in the rational planning approach.

Another writer in this vein is Van de Ven (1988) who identifies four problem areas, similar to Kanter's phases:

- Managing attention. An innovation is triggered by someone perceiving a problem, which might be some incongruence, some need that is not satisfied, or a change in the environment. Such problems are sources of opportunities but it is usually difficult to "see" the opportunity in the problem. Therefore, Van de Ven suggests that it is helpful to stand back from normal day-to-day activities and their taken-for-granted certainty in order to "see" differently. This is a cognitive problem and innovation is a creative way of understanding some reality. It involves a shifting of perspectives.
- Managing ideas. Once an individual has perceived a problem-opportunity, the next step is to persuade others to pursue it. Although, in this phase, people may be focusing on financial criteria, the process is primarily political as people negotiate financial backing and use cashflow figures to justify their positions. This is a political problem, in which the problem-solution must be acknowledged and validated by other people within the organization.
- Managing part–whole relationships. This is the activity of coordinating the inter-departmental activities and local interests; Van de Ven thinks about such coordination in terms of cybernetic systems. This is a managerial problem since, if an agreement to act is achieved, actions must be co-coordinated in order to succeed in realizing the solution.
- Institutional leadership. Shared cultures and compelling visions are prescribed to control behaviour and impart organizational coherence. This is a human interaction problem and leaders play a crucial role in drawing together the previous phases.

Designing the conditions

Writers in this tradition are claiming that while it may not be possible to control and manage innovations, it is possible to design and control the contextual and organizational conditions that enhance the probability of innovation occurring (Quinn, 1991). Kanter (1988) asserts that even though innovation is primarily a political and uncertain process, it is nevertheless subject to contextual conditions that can be managed to foster innovation.

It is important to notice how the above accounts of the requirements for innovation to take place are given from the perspective of the observer who objectively identifies the micro dynamics within and between the groups that make up an organization. This implies that it is possible for the researcher to stand outside those dynamics, evaluate them, and prescribe the "right behaviours" for innovation to occur, including the "right" kind of political action in the ongoing political battles identified as an essential part of the innovation process. This position is essentially also that prescribed for the leader. It becomes the leader's responsibility to install the "right" culture, so enfolding into a system the behavioural conditions required for innovation to occur. In my view, the problem with this reasoning is as follows. It is said that the cultural system functions in a way that secures behaviour decided in advance to be necessary for innovation, and that it operates as a form of control in that people will be compelled by peer pressure to conform to it. This kind of system is, by definition, incapable of producing anything genuinely new. Its whole purpose is to unfold what has already been enfolded in it. This aspect of the theory that writers like Kanter and Van de Ven adhere to, therefore cannot explain the origins of novelty. It can only explain how a novel idea already put into the system is unfolded. The origins of the novel idea have to be explained in another way and this other way is the vision of the charismatic leader or the subversive entrepreneurial individual. However, there is no explanation of how the leader or entrepreneur comes to such novel ideas and formulates them as visions to be put into the system.

There is also a contradiction in the argument. The leader designs the values for the cultural system and the purpose of this system is to ensure coherence in the organization through the peer pressure for conformity. However, another key feature of the explanation is that the leader as entrepreneur, or anyone else as entrepreneur, is described in heroic terms as one who defies the formal and legitimate system. In one role they conform and then these very same people subvert the system. The authors taking this position do not argue that they have in mind a paradoxical process. Instead, they simply eliminate the paradox by thinking in "both ... and" terms: there is *both* a formative cultural system of which leaders/entrepreneurs are parts, along with everyone else and autonomous leaders/entrepreneurs standing outside the system and operating on it. First, the leaders/entrepreneurs are thought of in one way and then in another way in a kind of figure–ground mode of thinking. It is this "both ... and" thinking that enables one not to notice the paradox and so eliminate it (Griffin, 2001). Furthermore, there is no explanation of how leaders/entrepreneurs come to occupy this external position or how they come to know what the required values are, or how they come to have novel ideas that they can formulate as visions. What the authors are doing is postulating that culture/vision are first-order cybernetic systems and then ignoring the problem of participation this raises, as expressed in second-order cybernetics. Instead of accounting for how it is possible for some individuals to stand outside of participation and arrange the participation of others, Kanter, and those taking similar approaches to hers, in effect imply a kind of mysticism. They assume that new meaning will emerge in some individual head because it has happened before, but how it happens is a mystery. They propose visions and values triggering enthusiastic engagement in political processes as an alternative to rationality. Visions and culture is the corner stone of this perspective, but they are external to the dynamics of interaction between people.

The first strand of thinking about innovation, reviewed above, regarded "innovation" as the primary goal, or intention, of an organization in a rapidly changing environment. To realize this intention, managers were required to take a strategic position and continuously "scan" the turbulent environment. The implication is that people in organizations can detect changes in advance, despite the great speed at which they are occurring, and can then rapidly reflect them in new products, new ways of organizing and new systems. All these "automatic" activities do not resonate with the experience of every day life. We do not change old habits automatically. We are not able to "align" ourselves rationally or find increasingly better cognitive "devices". In my view, these normative prescriptions simply lead to great anxiety and feelings of incompetence. Moving to the second strand, the prescriptions abandon the highly rational flavour of the first strand and propose much more spontaneous activity. However, they suggest that it is possible to design a system for such spontaneity. Ultimately these prescriptions simply lead to the "be spontaneous" paradox described by Watzlawick *et al.* (1967), which requires that a person act in direct contradiction to the order, so establishing a classic "double bind": be creative, but be creative according to the pre-given vision and values. Despite it's centring in the autonomous individual, this way of thinking ultimately denies human freedom by subjecting individuals to systemic imperatives.

The evidence

What is the evidence backing up the prescriptions presented by the two strands of thinking about innovation reviewed in this chapter? Some examples are the following. In support of the rational planning prescriptions, Zirger and Maidique (1990) researched 330 cases and claim to have identified major themes characterizing successful innovations: excellence of management, that is, careful planning of all phases and the coordination and integration of departments; value for customers; strategic focus; management commitment; market pioneering. Similar conclusions were drawn in studies by Johne and Snelson (1990), Cooper and Kleinschmidt (1991), Gupta and Wilemon (1990) and Crawford (1991). However, in support of the visions and values prescriptions, Kanter (1984, 1989) also analysed hundreds of case studies to deny most of the rational planning conclusions and claim empirical validation for her prescriptions. Furthermore, both sets of researchers often base their claims on the same case studies. Which are we to understand as the "true" version? The literature is full of success stories but there is little mention of dead-ends, the termination of projects and the catastrophic failures. Furthermore, most of the success stories are not told by those who were actually involved and, even when they are, they are often retrospectively presented in a favourable, rational light.

Conclusion

It has become commonplace to talk about innovation in terms of rational decision making based on foresight, where the main focus is the *system for decision making* and the outcome of those decisions, that is, on *an innovation*. One of the main points I want to make in this book, drawing on detailed account of innovation experiences, is that currently dominant ways of thinking about innovation *reify the system and the innovation*. This perspective is justified by appealing to hindsight and rationalizations of how particular innovations came to be. The effect is then to distract attention from the ongoing, ordinary and messy *processes* of innovation and this, in my view, leads us up several dead-ends rather than contributing to our understanding of what innovation is and how it comes about.

In the next chapter, I tell the story of a particular innovation and reflect on how it reveals the limitations of thinking about innovation processes in the way mainstream thought proposes.

3 The role of the individual in the process of innovation

- Oliveira's story of innovative concrete pipes
- The role of the individual
- Networks of conversations
- Conclusion

In the last chapter, I explored two prominent strands in mainstream thinking about innovation. The first strand, founded in the thought of neoclassical economics, understands innovation to originate in the mind of the autonomous individual. That individual is assumed to produce innovative ideas through processes of rational, deductive reasoning about market needs and the goals that the innovation must satisfy to meet those needs. These goals have to do with attaining optimal fit to market needs. Thereafter, the innovation proceeds according to a designed programme against which actual progress is monitored to secure the efficient realization of the innovation's goals. I pointed to how this is a "both ... and" way of thinking, in that the innovation process involves *both* the autonomous individual, understood as the rational chooser of the innovation and its goals, *and* a cybernetic or self-regulating system controlling the progress of the innovation so as to ensure its efficient realization. The emphasis is on efficiency understood as the removal of redundant, that is, unnecessary or surplus activity. The cybernetic or self-regulating system essentially damps difference to keep the innovation moving towards its goals. Deviations, instability and mess are all to be removed by the operation of the system. There is no place for variety or anything that might look like randomness or chance. Understanding is central and misunderstanding is in no way essential. Misunderstanding does not arise between rational individuals and when it does it is simply an inefficient distraction, or noise. The essence is removing uncertainty and securing stability and regularity. The system operates to keep activity moving towards a goal set from outside the system by the innovator, who takes the position of the objective observer in much the same way as the natural scientist, a rational, calculating forecaster. What is lacking in this way of thinking, I suggested, is an explanation of how the need for an innovation arises in the first place. The innovative idea is taken as a given, awaiting discovery by the reasoning processes of the autonomous individual. After this, the innovation proceeds automatically within a self-regulating system.

The second strand of thinking about innovation contests this highly rational planned view of how innovations come about and proposes an explanation that has its roots in the evolutionary economics of Schumpeter. The origin of an innovation is still understood in terms of the autonomous individual, but now that individual is the heroic, intuitive entrepreneur, who challenges existing ways of thinking and doing, even subverting current legitimate structures. This entrepreneur formulates the innovative idea as a vision and then engages in political processes to realize that vision. Linked to this idea of the heroic entrepreneur fighting to realize an innovative vision is the need for a cultural system that makes such entrepreneurial activity possible. It is postulated that the design of such a facilitative culture, expressed as a leadership vision, is the responsibility of charismatic leaders. The system in question, then, is not the cybernetic one of the rational school of thought, but the kind of systems dynamics, functional system to be found in Parsons's systemic sociology and Schein's view of culture. Control here is secured not by the automatic operation of monitoring activities but by the conformity of organizational members to the visions and values designed into the cultural system. Implicitly, people are then parts of a system and their interactions are an unfolding of the values and vision already enfolded into the system. This perspective stresses uncertainty. It is about social interaction understood as a system. Redundant diversity and misunderstanding trigger political interaction, which removes them.

Despite the differences in mechanism of control, both perspectives hold that it is possible to purposefully "design" the innovation process as the right sequence of tasks, in the rational planning perspective, and the right visions, structures and cultures, in the entrepreneurial/social perspective. Furthermore, although the entrepreneurial view of innovation differs markedly from the rational view, it retains the "both . . . and" structure of thought. There is still *both* the autonomous individual as entrepreneur and as leader who takes the position of objective observer *and* the cultural and political system. There is still no explanation of how innovative ideas arise in the first place. The explanation starts once an entrepreneur has an innovative idea. Thereafter the process is one of unfolding the enfolded idea. There is also a contradiction between the cultural system of conformity proposed and the picture of the entrepreneur as one who reacts against conformity.

Having noted the theoretical difficulties in both strands of thinking about innovation, I then pointed, in the last chapter, to the conflicting evidence as each school of thought produces case studies, often the same ones, to support its prescriptions.

In this chapter, I want to explore the experience of a particular innovator called Martins de Oliveira. In 1992, Professor Fernando Gonçalves was in charge of the launching of Lisbon's Science Park. Gonçalves knew of the concrete drainage galleries Oliveira was developing, and decided to use that system in the science park. Gonçalves had, as a member of the science and technology board, supported Oliveira before, when he applied for some funds to pursue his work. I was studying under Professor Gonçalves's supervision at the time and he thought that Oliveira's innovation would make an interesting case for my studies. So he introduced me to Oliveira and I interviewed him. Since then, we have met and talked together on many occasions. In the rest of this section I recount what I have learned about the process of innovation that Oliveira has been involved in. I am not producing this story as evidence for one perspective on the innovation process rather than another. I am not suggesting that it constitutes "evidence". Rather, it is a story that Oliveira and many others I talked to told me. The story is, of course, interpreted by me in accordance with my own personal, subjective ways of understanding. I think a story such as this invites the reader to consider how it resonates or fails to resonate with the two strands of mainstream thinking reviewed in the last chapter. For me, the story points to ways to think about innovation other than the mainstream.

Oliveira's story of innovative concrete pipes

In the winter of 1983, Martins de Oliveira, a civil engineer, was appointed by the city council of Sintra to assess the damage to its newly commissioned sewage system caused by severe flooding during the winter. The drainpipe component of this system consisted of circular concrete pipe sections, each section sealed against the other by means of a rubber ring. To carry out his task, he used aerial photographs to document in detail the massive destructive power of the flood. He found that the pipeline was totally inoperative: over large areas the water had completely uncovered and ripped apart the pipes, bridges were destroyed, and the water had displaced tons of earth and rocks. Later, Oliveira showed the photographs he had taken to a seminar at the Technical University of Lisbon. He was surprised when the head of the Hydraulics Department, Professor Quintela, told him that the rainfall during the flood of 1968 had been even greater than in 1983. He was surprised because his survey had shown that the water had risen to levels above those of previous floods and the damage caused was much more severe. Why were the flooding and the damage more severe when the rainfall was lower? He took the view that haphazard construction of buildings near streams might have changed natural riverbanks, hence the higher water levels, but that this could not account for the extent of the damage to the drainage system.

Why did he reach this conclusion? He noticed that the concrete pipes had not been able to contain the internal turbulent flow of water. The erosion provoked by the pressure of water within the concrete pipes was striking: it was as if someone had been hammering and carving the pipes for a long time. The sealing rubber rings had been pushed out from the inside on the upper part of the pipes. The explanation, therefore, for what had happened was simple enough. The joints had not been able to stand the internal pressure and vibration caused by the turbulent flow of a forceful and excessive volume of water. Furthermore, land displacements had damaged the structure causing some sections to separate from each other. The circular concrete pipe is a classic solution to drainage problems that has been used for a long time. Engineering schools teach that there is a direct relationship between the pipe diameter and the volume of water it can accommodate in a given time period. Such systems are not designed to withstand dynamically turbulent overflows that lead the pipes to vibrate, nor are they designed to stand flexor movements provoked by land displacements.

After graduating, Oliveira's first job had been in Hidrotécnica, a leading civil engineering company working on large projects such as drainage systems, dams, and roads. He knew that drainage systems are not designed to cope with turbulent flows of liquids, as in a flood situation when the pipes operate on an overcharge regime. So, Oliveira wondered how to solve this problem. In conversations with his colleagues, they all kept returning to the rubber joints. What materials could be used to prevent the uneven pressure? Could the ring be designed to fit in a different way? For the next six months, Oliveira tried a number of different solutions to the rubber joint problem, in between carrying out his other duties as head of the technical department of the city council of Sintra. However, he had little success since none of the materials seemed to be able to prevent the destruction of the rings. While he was engaging in his informal experiments with different materials, the replacement of the pipeline began. New circular pipe sections with rubber rings replaced the damaged ones.

Oliveira visited the works during the replacement project and was surprised to find that the new concrete pipes were transported from Coimbra some 200 kilometres away, despite the fact that there were many local manufacturers able to supply the same pipes. Furthermore, the circular shape of the pipes meant that each lorry could only carry 6 metres of pipeline, with enormous waste of transportation capacity. He soon found out why the pipes were being transported from so far away. The Coimbra supplier was selling at very low prices because of financial difficulties and this offset the higher transport costs.

The idea

Oliveira felt frustrated by both the failure of his tests of possible substitutes for the rubber rings and the waste of transportation capacity. He was about to abandon the whole issue when he came across a description, in an engineering book he was reading, of sewage systems developed during the Roman Empire. These were oval galleries that were large enough to allow maintenance visits, an issue he was particularly sensitive to since it was part of his daily tasks. He began to wonder why circular shapes were dominant in modern systems. He also began to wonder whether it would be possible to manufacture pipe sections in longitudinal rather then vertical section in such way that they could be easily assembled on site. This would allow more sections to be loaded onto a lorry, so improving the utilization of transport capacity. When he started talking to his colleagues about these ideas, they dismissed them outright. They did not consider it part of their role as municipal engineers to get involved in matters of design, manufacture and transport. They only listened to him at all because he was the head of the department. Nevertheless, he went on talking about developing oval pipes made of three parts with longitudinal joints sealed with some kind of silicone, despite knowing that circular concrete pipes were easier to produce.

He was also considering whether the oval pipe shape could tolerate the stress generated by liquid overflows. Much to his children's amusement he started using chocolate boxes and chocolate wrapping papers to construct models of three-part pipelines. One of the reasons for this kind of makeshift experimentation at his home was the scepticism, even ridicule, of his colleagues. This went on for quite some time, until he was quite pleased with the "models" and "prototypes" he had built. He kept showing these models to people and, eventually, he attracted some attention. To the dismay of some of his relatives, he left a "perfectly steady job for an impossible adventure", namely, the design and manufacture of oval pipes.

"The research"

In the spring of 1985, after leaving the city council's technical services, he applied for a patent for his concept of a three-part pipe with a longitudinal joint. The pipes were designed not only for drainage, but also to carry electricity cables, telephone and TV cables, gas pipes, water pipes and other subterranean distribution systems. However, he was still not able to justify scientifically the use of oval shapes because he lacked the mathematical knowledge to simulate their properties. In late 1985, therefore, he applied for a grant from the government Board for Scientific and Technological Research to fund engineering research of pipe dynamics. In support of this application, he supplied the Board with a file of photographs illustrating his technical concepts. Since his father had been the Vice President of the National Laboratory for Civil Engineering, he emphasized his surname. He also stressed his long career, hoping that this would encourage Board members to take him seriously, something which he found few were doing. He got the grant and this allowed him to devote his full-time attention to his project – the study of an optimized shape for drainage pipes that could endure the turbulence and vibration generated by floods or earthquakes. In order to receive this grant Oliveira had to establish a private company. So, with his wife, he set up a company called Mobel, initially with a very small capital base.

The next three years were spent mostly at home, muddling through every possible parameter affecting the ideal oval pipe shape. A number of variables were examined and progressively abandoned, leaving only the depth at which the pipe was to be laid, the nature of the ground, and the diameter of the pipe. Oliveira concluded that the first two of these variables represented the opposing forces that induce folding movements in the pipes, and that pipes behaved differently according to their dimensions when submitted to those forces. The depth at which the pipe is laid relates to the vertical stress to which it is submitted, the weight of land above it, and the mobile charges passing on top of it, for instance, railways and roads. The nature of the ground relates to the horizontal stress to which it is submitted: some soils present expansion pressures, while others, for example, stony soils, do not.

At this point, Oliveira faced the problem of the ideal shape for any given dimension of pipe, assuming that the two opposing forces would cancel each other out. Since he did not possess the computational means or the knowledge to build a program to do the calculations, he hired some engineering companies to develop the mathematical calculations and simulations for his analysis. After some months, two of these companies had made no progress and were increasingly sceptical of his ideas. One of them said: "What you request is not in the books."

Finally, he and Luis Azevedo, who had taught him at university and was a partner in a small engineering company, developed a program in Basic to simulate the behaviour of pipes under the influence of the three variables mentioned above. Six hundred curves were generated as optimal shapes in different conditions, but such a large range of optimal shapes raised many problems, including how they might be manufactured. Four months were spent working on this problem. Oliveira reports that spirits were not high during this time and, even though prizes in international exhibitions for inventions were awarded for his pipes, he considered abandoning his endeavour on account of the apparent dead-end to which his 600 optimal shapes were heading. He felt his pipes were ideal but of little economic interest. At his former university faculty, he was playing with long series of graphic displays of curves unable to find a common link between any of them. An array of strategies was used to try to solve this problem. However, none of them provided a solution.

Then in a casual meeting in the faculty bar, Oliveira complained to Professor Valadas Fernandes about the standstill his research had reached. The professor suggested that operational research had an answer and that Oliveira might consider calculating the envelope curve to those 600 curves. Professor Fernandes pointed out that he had taught Oliveira, many years ago, how to do this. Oliveira took his advice and calculated the form of the curve that condensed all the others; this provided him with the form of the mould that could be used to manufacture all the pipes.

After this problem was solved, with the cooperation and support of the National Laboratory of Civil Engineering, prototypes were tested in a department where earthquakes and their effects on buildings and structures are simulated. This testing proved that the shapes Oliveira invented were in fact the most resistant to the kind of forces pipes are submitted to under earthquake or overcharge regimes.

Does the story so far resonate with the rational planning perspective on innovation? The answer to this question, I think, is "yes and no". There was certainly a great deal of reasoning. There was a goal. However, the goal had emerged as a passion in Oliveira's daily activities. Furthermore, he did not know where he was going with the idea. In other words, he had no overall plan. Each solution uncovered other "problems", which in turn might become opportunities. One could hardly describe the process as efficient. On the contrary, there were many activities that turned out to be redundant. There was misunderstanding, his and others, and it was an essential trigger to what he did next. Instead of a global plan, there was only local action in the living present.

Does the story so far resonate any better with the entrepreneurial/social perspective on the innovation process? Again, the answers seems to me to be "yes and no". Oliveira was a rather heroic, stubborn, even subversive individual. Politics and informal networks of contacts certainly played a very important part in how the innovation evolved. However, one can hardly say that Oliveira operated within a supportive cultural system that some charismatic leader had designed. There were no charismatic leaders to be seen. There was no mentor or product champion, but there were a number of people who contributed in conversations with Oliveira to the evolution of the innovative idea. Indeed, the key feature of the development of this innovation was the conversational interaction between Oliveira and others in local situations in the living present.

Consider now how the story developed.

The company

In the winter of 1988, after obtaining a new patent for the process of manufacturing his pipes and technical galleries, he started looking for partners. He thought that existing companies working in the area of prefabricated concrete might be interested in the opportunity to create a market niche and would be willing to supply the commercial and the manufacturing capabilities. His approaches met with no success. Finally,

Oliveira found a company in the area of Sintra, which lent him space and facilities.

This company was known for its innovative spirit but was going through a difficult financial period and had no resources to commit to a new product. Nevertheless, they were willing to let him use some of their space. It was here that the mould of the first section of pipeline with a variable radius curve shape was constructed. Using maritime plywood to build the moulds, Oliveira and a group of workers built the first 600 metres of pipe for a project commissioned by Carlos Pimenta, the secretary of state of environmental issues. Carlos Pimenta had met Oliveira in Brussels, at the inventions exhibition where he received a prize. Although the secretary of state wished to give Oliveira the whole job, his senior civil servants argued that the new kind of pipeline was too experimental and so Oliveira was given only 600 metres, a small part of the whole project.

The financial difficulties facing Oliveira's host company increased and he could see that he could not go on using expensive handcrafted moulds. So, in the winter of 1989, he drew together all the financial resources he could and acquired land near Pinhal Novo, just south of Lisbon. He approached the largest Portuguese bank for a loan to build manufacturing facilities for his company on this site. The Portuguese State owns this bank and, in addition to its normal commercial activity, it was used as a tool of economic policy. Some years before, this bank had funded two competitions for innovative industrial products and Oliveira had won them both with his pipes and manufacturing process. The bank had also sponsored his presence in international competitions. However, bank officials told him that other variables are involved in the progress from invention to market. Although they believed in his technical and manufacturing expertise, they felt it was necessary for him to bring other partners into the venture with the "required managerial capabilities". They would then feel more comfortable in considering a possible loan.

Oliveira introduced businessmen he knew who were willing to join the project. However, the bank politely refused to consider them on the grounds that even though they were successful entrepreneurs, they did not possess any expertise in the area of concrete prefabrication or in the civil engineering industry. Oliveira then approached the major cement companies. Again, he had no success. So, he turned to a venture capital company called SulPedip, which had recently been formed by the government to promote innovative industrial activities and innovation based start-ups. Here his project was well received but once again he was told that he had to have a partner; they stipulated that the partner should be Engil, one of the three major civil construction companies in Portugal. Oliveira opposed the idea of having a partner who was also a potential customer because of the effect it might have on other potential customers. However, in 1991 he conceded and sold part of Mobel to Engil and SulPedip, leaving him with a 40 per cent stake.

The manufacturing process

The product innovation led to a process innovation. Rather than the traditional way of manufacturing concrete products, where there is a mould for each product size, Oliveira thought that the optimized shapes and their envelope curve might allow him to ask a different question. How many sizes might be manufactured with one mould? This led him to create a universal mould to manufacture all his pipes. This mould is an ingenious piece of engineering, since it involves a flexible sliding system that allows the manufacturing of different sizes just by means of a mechanical reduction of the mould. In fact, with only one mould it is possible to produce pipes ranging from 1 to 5 metres, with any diameter in between. Having discovered that his mould sliding system was capable of producing variations in shape, he then explored the possibility of manufacturing other products. Various experiments led to a number of patented products, ranging from wave deflectors to sound barriers for motorways and bus stop shelters.

The take-off

While he was negotiating with the bank and trying to get partners for Mobel, Oliveira obtained another small contract in the winter of 1990. This time, the order was for 800 metres of technical gallery for a new university campus in Lisbon. This gallery was to carry the entire infrastructure required for several buildings for the new campus of the Science Faculty. These pipes were manufactured without a gantry, a crane, or a mixing system. The moulds were laid on the ground by hand and the concrete was produced by a small portable concrete mixer and filled in manually. By 1992, Mobel was a reality. The construction of the factory building was complete and all the necessary equipment had been acquired. The company was established with a manufacturing capability of 130 cubic metres of prefabricated concrete on an 8-hour shift and this placed Mobel among the top companies in the sector.

However, the new Mobel's first contract had nothing to do with pipelines and galleries. In 1991, at Figueira da Foz, a coastal town with an extensive sandy beach located some 200 kilometres north of Lisbon, there was a plan to build a road along the northern part of the seashore. This was no minor problem since the ocean in this area systematically erodes the coastal sands and, therefore, the construction of 300 metres of vertical wall was required in order to prevent the erosion that endangered the road. However, this would mean the destruction of a beautiful grove of tamarisks, as well as the disappearance of a small adjacent beach and the destruction of natural barriers to the strong northern wind that would make the large beach even more unpleasant on windy days. Oliveira was a regular visitor to that small beach and was upset by the proposed wall. During a weekend at Figueira da Foz, he discussed the matter with the President of the Municipal Chamber and both agreed that an alternative should be studied.

Oliveira came back to Mobel and started pondering on what could be done about this problem. He did not know much about maritime hydraulics or about the specifics of civil engineering of this kind of work. However, he talked to several friends in Hidrotécnica, his employer of many years ago, the Engineering Faculty at the university and other institutions about the issue and became more informed about the theoretical and practical implications of construction in seashore areas. Also, since he used to dive in those areas, he knew something about ocean floors and the currents. He had one conversation after another with scientists and academics in the institutions that had helped him before. His aim was to find a way of ensuring land stability for the road while leaving as much as possible of the environment untouched.

Several methods were suggested by his scientist friends, many of whom asked to remain anonymous since, once again, their suggestions were highly experimental and not to be found in respectable engineering books. There was no time to conduct a rigorous applied research project, which in any case did not "fit" Oliveira's approach. He went back to his own makeshift experiments: for example, one method that emerged in conversations with his scientist friends involved throwing sand coloured with nail polish to observe and record the movements induced by currents and wave breaking to identify patterns of erosion. Finally, in late 1991, he proposed a solution that looked anything but stable and capable of resisting the tides. Instead of a compact wall, he designed a structure comprising a set of "L" shaped pieces of concrete (developed in previous experiments for which he had found no use) laid over the sand in layers to form a kind of ladder. At the bottom of the ladder, which was most affected by the direct action of the waves, there was an elliptical wall that caused the waves to roll over themselves on breaking, so preventing the tides from dragging sand into the ocean.

Much to Oliveira's surprise, after a short process of analysis by various governmental and local authorities, the go-ahead was given. The construction of the structure and of the road was completed in 1992. This is indeed surprising considering that Portugal is not particularly well known for rapid decision making processes, especially when different layers of the public administration are involved and certainly in relation to innovative concepts. Oliveira points out that the most likely explanation was the fact that several of the people involved in the decision making process were born in the town whose environment was being threatened. They all shared the common concerns of love for that small beach and distaste for the visual and ecological impact of structures on seashores.

Needless to say, Oliveira also patented this solution and once again he was awarded prizes. This structure proved to be erosion resistant and well concealed when the tamarisk trees grew again. In fact, the structure had survived undamaged by two of the most severe winters of the last forty years, while other classically constructed structures suffered significant damage. This was an innovative approach but not without risk. Oliveira himself thought it was risky at the time and he recalls people making bets on how soon the whole thing would be taken away by the waves.

Notice how much the evolution of Oliveira's business depended upon other people and other organizations. What struck me as the story unfolded was how opportunities arose and difficulties were dealt with in ordinary conversational interaction in local situations in the living present. Sometimes what seemed to be a waste of effort, what seemed to be redundant, turned out to have a use after all. It is striking how Oliveira was taking all kinds of risks without knowing what the consequences would be. Throughout, however, there were continuing elements of rational planning and there was the kind of stubborn determination of the entrepreneur, as well as the intense political activity typical of the entrepreneurial/social perspective on innovation. Perhaps one can begin to see how both the rational planning and the entrepreneurial/social explanations of the innovation process focus attention on aspects of what is a much wider process of communicative interaction.

The setbacks

Shortly after the work done for the Science Park of Lisbon, Oliveira's partners failed to nominate any board members. This meant that he was not able to operate bank accounts since this required two signatures on behalf of Mobel. The reason for Engil's involvement in the first place was to contribute to Mobel's business development but, instead of doing this, on several occasions Engil proposed to acquire Oliveira's patents or his shares in Mobel. In November 1995, he finally bought the shares of the other two partners. Oliveira claims that his innovative products and his innovative process had lowered the prices of prefabricated cement pieces but that others in the industry were not all that interested. When I talked to people from the industry, they told me that they were more interested in increasing sales turnover than in increasing margins. Oliveira's efforts had not found favour with them because his products reduced contract sizes in financial terms. Perhaps for this reason, none of the big construction companies ever demonstrated an interest in his products. After the launch of Mobel, two major national projects requiring technical galleries were announced. These were a new bridge across the river Tagus and facilities for the world exhibition of 1998. However, no company showed any interest in Oliveira's proposals, even though his costs were considerably lower than the competition. Oliveira complained that the powerful companies were boycotting him. Then, in the winter of 1996, severe storms destroyed the beach walls at Figueira da Foz, except for the part built using Oliveira's technique. However, this had little impact on his detractors who simply ignored him. Perhaps the oval galleries would be all over Portugal by now if Oliveira had agreed to sell his patents to the big companies.

After 1995, Oliveira found it impossible to meet the financial agreement made with the banks; just when it seemed that they would force him to accept the offers of the construction companies, he came up with the idea of using the ground adjacent to the plant for real estate development. Ironically, the success of this venture owed much to the new bridge, where his galleries had been turned down, because they brought Pinhal Novo "closer" to Lisbon. In the years since then, Oliveira has survived by licensing his products, particularly his bus stop shelters, to a company in Braga. This company has manufactured some hundreds of these shelters for several town councils around that area. More recently, some town councils have been trying to have their towns classified as "world heritage sites" by UNESCO. As part of qualifying for this, they are considering the use of Oliveira's galleries to conceal every cable, TV antenna and pipe that is now disfiguring buildings, walls and roof tops in the historical centres of these towns. Also, use of the galleries would prevent continual re-opening of holes and ditches in historical parts of these towns. In one of these cities, Evora, Oliveira's technical galleries are to be used as visiting points whenever an artefact or any other archaeological object is found and it is decided against its removal from the original location. The architects and archaeologists who favour the galleries for the above reasons have to fight internal battles with their engineering colleagues who still favour traditional solutions. Some enthusiastically adopt Oliveira's views, but in other areas he is firmly excluded.

Oliveira firmly believes that the function of the engineer is to provide the best possible solution at the lowest possible price. However, apparently this is not the central theme organizing the behaviour of other participants in the industry. Oliveira publicly challenges the results of bids and attacks both financial and technical criteria used in the decision processes by public authorities. According to one engineering consultant, his personality stands in the way of his own success. He is reported as being biased in favour of his creations, too inflexible to play a game that has some less clear rules, namely, involving over-invoicing on government contracts. Oliveira speaks quite openly of what he calls "corruption and scandals" in the industry and this confrontational attitude does not make him a very popular person in the community of civil construction.

The developments just described bring out, for me, some very important aspects of the process of communicative interaction between people in which innovations emerge. These aspects are to do with power, not simply as political processes of negotiation but as group process of inclusion and exclusion. Innovation always changes patterns of action, and changes in patterns of action always amount to shifts in figurations of power relations. Those who sense that they could lose out in such shifts are bound to respond in ways that seek to maintain power differentials in their favour and these responses will tend to exclude those whose ideas threaten existing patterns of power relations. These patterns of power relations do not arise in some system outside of the interaction between people but, rather, emerge in the ordinary relating between people in local situations in the living present. It is notable how Oliveira continually responds to the gestures made by others, all in the local situations of their interaction.

I am not claiming that the account I have given of Oliveira's innovations is in any way objective evidence that can support one theory of the innovation process and disprove others. Rather, I am trying to explore how I might make sense of the innovation process as I came to understand it in my relationship with Oliveira.

I could try to make sense of this experience from one or both of the two strands of mainstream thinking that I identified in Chapter 2. Indeed there is much in the experience that one might select to support the rational planning perspective. After all, Oliveira was an engineer and he behaved like a rational engineer in many respects. You could argue that he approached the design of pipelines in a typical engineering fashion, identifying a technical need, conducting experiments and making calculations and experimenting with prototypes. Indeed he did all of these. On the other hand, you could point to the intense political activity in which he had to engage in order to get anywhere with his project. You could also describe Oliveira as a typical individual entrepreneur, a product champion, who worked in messy intuitive ways to develop his vision. You could point to the obstacles he encountered because of the obstructive culture he found himself operating in, and you could claim that this suggests the need to design a more supportive culture if innovation is to flourish. Indeed there is much in Oliveira's story to support an interpretation from the kind of perspective that Kanter and others take. No wonder, then, that each side is able to take the same case studies and claim support in them for their perspective. Alternatively you could take both perspectives and argue that the experience is best understood as *both* rational planning *and* entrepreneurial activity.

However, it seems to me that, while each of these perspectives, separately and together, illuminate much that happened, there are important aspects that they miss. To start with, consider how these perspectives on innovation encourage an almost exclusive focus on the autonomous individual, either as rational calculator or as heroic, intuitive entrepreneur.

The role of the individual

As I have said, it could be argued that Oliveira's story "fits" the classical notion of the entrepreneur. Oliveira questioned taken-for-granted assumptions about the shape of sewage ducts. As Van de Ven (1988) claims of innovators, he "paid attention" to problems that no one else seemed to think existed. When confronted with the damage caused by the flood, he did not behave as others did, ascribing the damage to the newly constructed sewage system to the forces of nature or blaming contractors for poor quality work. He did not immediately start calculating how much it would cost to replace the system. Instead, again as Van de Ven claims, he "perceived an incongruence and redefined the situation" by treating the duct shape as part of the problem. Furthermore, he was willing to act on his views despite his colleagues' jokes about his "crazy" notion of questioning the round shape of the ducts. In this sense, he could be said to fit the archetype of Kirton's (1980) innovator.

However, this perspective focuses only on what he was able to "see", not why he was able to perceive the problem–opportunity from a different angle to that of his colleagues. To understand why he was able to do this, one must take account of his previous experiences in which emerged the diversity of his frames of reference as well as his ability to bear the anxiety of conflicting views. Early on in his career, it was part of his role to mediate between engineers and architects who had very different concerns, often conflicting ones, in relation to the projects for which they shared responsibility. During his career in the city council, he had been responsible at various times for new project development, planning, construction and maintenance. In the course of these activities, he had acquired the ability to participate in many different perspectives, reflected in different ways of talking in the engineering and other communities. Even his hobbies were relevant. For instance, his hobby of scuba diving was instrumental in solving practical, yet critical, problems on the project of the beach wall. In other words, Oliveira's abilities were not given qualities, simply possessed by him, which one can label as "entrepreneurial". He did not make himself. What he was, what he found himself able to do, had emerged in the long process of his relating to many others over many years.

A central feature of relating, of interaction between people, is the conversations they continually engage in. One could argue, therefore, that what Oliveira found himself doing emerged in his ongoing communicative interaction, his conversations, with others. In this sense there is no beginning to innovation. Indeed it becomes problematic to call it "his" innovation. What became "his" innovation was emerging in the many conversations he had with others both before the events I recount above and during them. It is striking how many of the conversations during the period I deal with above were characterized by misunderstanding. Initially, his colleagues in Sintra misunderstood the potential of oval pipes. Perhaps he misunderstood the need for management input. Perhaps the financiers pressing him to involve professional managers misunderstood the relevance of this to the work Oliveira was doing.

As they engaged with each other over the period, it is the continual differences between people's views that are striking, not what they "shared" in conformity with a shared culture. Furthermore, it is clear that the interactions between Oliveira and many others cannot be described as efficient. There was much duplication and repetition. In other words the communicative interactions were characterized by redundancy – from the viewpoint of efficiency, messy, repetitive interactions are not necessary. For example, he developed "L" shaped concrete sections and then could find no use for them until much later when a project he could not have foreseen at the time emerged. He generated 600 pipe shapes, which he did not know how to use at first. He probably never had any use for most of the shapes. He messed about with chocolate boxes in trying to develop pipe shapes. Looking back most of what he did now makes sense, but at the time it looked very inefficient, even unnecessary and so redundant. However, with hindsight one can see how small differences, diversity that seemed redundant, was to escalate into new ways of thinking. For example, even his scuba diving turned out to be relevant to developing the design of the sea wall. Other apparently small events also turned out to have amplified consequences, for example, when he refused to sell his patents to the concrete companies.

These themes of the role of conversation and redundant diversity/ misunderstanding as essential to the innovation process will be developed in subsequent chapters.

Was Oliveira the kind of entrepreneur the literature encourages us to believe in? Certainly, the galleries became a powerful personal quest. You could call this a vision. However, this immediately implies a kind of knowing, a kind of clarity and certainty that I think he never really had, at least not until well into the evolution of his story. As soon as one thinks that the innovations were realizations of Oliveira's "vision" one unrealistically ascribes to him the power of choosing how his ideas would materialize; this then distracts attention from the continuing role others played. In other words, the hindsight tendency to ascribe what happens to someone's intentional choice immediately covers over the messy uncertain process of communicative interaction, with its power dynamics of inclusion and exclusion, in which the innovation emerged.

Oliveira came to have a very strong reaction against the large companies. He felt that they had no respect for his work and that they mistreated him. His response was to set his own terms for a game that they would not play and the more he felt obstructed the more he stuck to his position. When I talked to people in these companies, I found that they thought he was far too stubborn and outspoken. This was not the idealization of the entrepreneur so often found in the literature. Instead there was an open power play with its dynamics of inclusion and exclusion. I was struck by how gossip was shaping events. What people were saying about Oliveira and what he was saying about them in gossipy conversations in many places was actually affecting what people then did. Fantasy played its part too. Indeed, to listen to Oliveira moving rapidly from what sounded like one unrealistic idea to another was to listen to someone powerfully elaborating his experience in imaginative ways that could even be called fantasy. In our first meetings, all kinds of incredible sounding projects were suggested with a sense of urgency, as if every one of these projects was actually on the move and being developed. Strong emotion also clearly played its part in how, why and what people were doing in the story I have recounted above. The process has an emotional dimension. Even though Oliveira is not very willing to value this dimension, he occasionally recognizes that his personal life was affected in multiple ways. He refers to personal vicissitudes in some phases and mentions his wife's emotional support when things seemed to be dark, although eventually they did get divorced. He also reports that during some phases, when the outcomes of his effort were not very clear, he experienced some distress. Close relatives and friends were concerned at what they described as his stubbornness and advised him to resume a rational course of action, meaning – get a proper job. These are all aspects of the process of communicative interaction in which innovation emerges.

However, despite the epic proportions of the story, its sadder epilogue and the fascinating individual traits of Oliveira, the evolution of this story does not rely solely on one individual. Oliveira contributed to the formation of this innovation but his own identity was also being formed by his innovation, to such an extent that after a while one cannot distinguish one process from the other.

Networks of conversations

Oliveira was able to establish connections with highly diverse groups of people. He had connections in the National Laboratories, the finance institutions, the Board of Scientific Research, city councils, government offices and companies. In the "conception phase" of the innovation, he was able to discuss his ideas with a variety of people and to obtain comments, information, critiques and suggestions from them. From his descriptions of the process only a few of these relationships were established through formal channels. The majority of them were informal and based on personal acquaintances formed throughout his career. He did not build this network of contacts intentionally and never knew when he would call on acquaintances from many years previously. He recognizes that through this informal network he participated in an effective process of sorting out problems and acquiring the information he needed. However, he often got more than he bargained for. Through these informal networks of conversations he also participated in other conversations in which problems were being addressed that he had never thought about, and that sometimes became business opportunities for his company.

What Oliveira did was not well tolerated in official circles. Some of the scientists he talked to actually demanded secrecy. Although they were enthusiastic about Oliveira's projects, they did not wish to be publicly associated with his unconventional approaches. However, Oliveira did receive support. For example, he was able to obtain funding to start his company. Government policy on innovation also turned out to be beneficial to him. For example, the establishment of venture capital companies proved to be helpful in gaining market attention for his ideas.

However, the emergence of new meaning cannot be guaranteed. After the "development phase", leading companies found that what he was doing threatened their positions. They took steps to protect the status quo, so blocking the emergence of new meaning. They sought to stop outsiders and newcomers from "rocking the boat". This pattern is also an illustration of how power differentials play a role in fostering or damping creativity, and how they underline the dynamics of exclusion of some people from ongoing conversations.

Oliveira's innovations threatened to change established practices and roles of too many: project companies, large contractors, and small subcontractors. I remember asking an official in the city council of Lisbon about the reason for not using the galleries, at least in new extensions. The response was another question: What would be the advantage? I suggested that it might be beneficial to avoid the need for frequently ripping up the streets of the capital each time some section of cable needed to be replaced. The official agreed but pointed out that many would resist this because it would make it too easy to monitor the quality of what was being buried! Contractors would not want to lay themselves open to demands for compensation for poor quality work. Some participants in these events, therefore, reacted as a group in order to defend what they perceived as a threat to their interests. From a political point of view, Oliveira responded by confronting them, assuming that everyone would understand his claims that the resisting interests were illegitimate. He felt that it was "obvious" that his solutions had great technical and economic superiority.

The process that led to the innovation was not linear nor was it planned. Several unintended outcomes and events, to which he was able to respond with different answers, shaped the final outcome. The trajectory was not simply the product of intention and of outlining the steps to be taken in advance of action, but of responding to local and concrete gestures, discovering of outcomes caused by chance or by other people's will and interest in the situations. He did not intend or predict that the mould would be such a powerful instrument of flexibility. The mould was actually, in the beginning, a by-product of his work. The moulding process is in itself a sort of virtuous cycle, and there is not yet a clear sense of what might be produced by using it. It is still in an ongoing phase of sensemaking (Weick, 1995) as Oliveira is playing with it. The moulding process was one unintended outcome that became a window of opportunity. The partners of Mobel were the result of other people's interests and goals, and the final arrangement to establish the company was a long way away from a desirable outcome from his point of view.

Mobel's innovative products were of interest to government and municipal authorities. Oliveira had the opportunity to discuss his innovations with many people and to persuade them that his technical galleries were a better solution than the conventional buried pipes. He showed how his approach would save money and avoid disrupting people's lives with needless holes and blockages in the streets and roads. Given his arguments, both political and scientific, most people tended to accept the beneficial nature of his innovations. However, he has failed to get his gallery concept prescribed by architects or engineers. It turns out that they are not impressed by a concept that was supposed to "save" them the trouble of opening ditches and holes in the ground. In addition, his innovation allowed easy maintenance of cables that would run in the galleries. Typically, the telephone, electricity, and TV companies subcontract cable laying to small companies. Oliveira found that these smaller companies were not very enthusiastic about his innovation either – obviously it would seriously reduce their work opportunities. Easy inspections mean easy assessment of the quality of cables used in the first place. His innovation had some threatening aspects since it would shift some of the rules of games that were played and with which most of the players were quite comfortable. Naturally, the objections to his innovation were not addressed in this way. Political processes of lobbying were used to cast serious doubts on the quality of his galleries. However, these tactics met a problem, since the state laboratory that certified his gallery is a reputable one and it is the one that civil engineering companies must call to be certified themselves. Thus, this line was of no consequence, and was replaced by another one. Questioning of the high cost of Oliveira's production was then pursued. Oliveira had by then successfully introduced the issue "technical gallery", so the solution is now to avoid his patented gallery. At the same time, he was trying to undermine the lobbies by approaching the press and political connections.

The opposing arguments are not conducted in the same pattern of talk as the one Oliveira uses. Others are not using physics or engineering to argue but sophisticated political tactics, for example, gossip: someone said that his products in some job were not without problems, not mentioning specifically what the problems were, nor who told them about them. Therefore, in the end, the innovation is conditioned by the product of the actions of all agents, both those that contributed to its development and those who refuse to accept it for various reasons. Oliveira's new products emerged out of a conflict between his views and the dominant political "regime" his innovation was supposed to fit into.

Conclusion

Although one might argue that the innovations discussed in this chapter were driven by an individual, it is clear that this individual's actions can only be understood within a much broader context. The process of innovation here was not primarily within one individual but the innovations were constantly emerging in processes of communicative interaction. The innovation process was in important ways an informal conversational process in which connections and diversity were of crucial importance. In the context of the city council technical department it is doubtful that Oliveira would have found the resources and the conversational dynamics he needed to develop his technical gallery. He needed to have access to a rich network of information, as well as the personal drive to sustain a process that led to high emotional and social pressures since he had a family and gave up his source of income. He was able to relate to people in different institutions which possessed the knowledge that was pertinent to his problems, and he did it in an informal way. Had he followed established official procedures it is debatable whether he would have arrived at his innovation in the time it took by way of his heuristic approach.

However, this story also gives some insight into other issues. These have to do with the redundant diversity and misunderstanding in the conversations Oliveira engaged in, the level of trust and the robustness of the patterns of talk Oliveira was able to participate in throughout his lifetime. In engaging in conversations about the drainage system, he was able to speculate about and to question long accepted assumptions, rather than engaging in the more "economic" and usual activity of figuring out how much replacing the system would cost and how "one could do more of the same but a bit better this time". A high level of trust connected him with those who have helped him along the way. If he had not been trusted, for instance, by those who engaged in the rather questionable venture of the seashore wall, he would not have been able to realize such a solution. The patterns of talk (dynamic patterns of meaning) Oliveira participated in, enabled him to understand the problems he faced and to engage in conversation with a variety of people. If Oliveira had not been a civil engineer he probably would not have been able to solve the problem. Nevertheless, if Oliveira had only participated in accepted engineering patterns of talk he might also never have perceived any problem and, even if he had, he probably would not have been able to solve it.

In the next chapter I will develop the points made about innovation in this chapter, only this time in relation to a story in which there is no clear individual entrepreneur.

4 The conversational nature of the innovation process

- The story of systems development at a water utility
- The absence of the heroic entrepreneur
- Power relations
- Conclusion

Some two years into my involvement with Oliveira and the development of his innovations, described in the last chapter, I joined a doctoral group at the University of Hertfordshire. The members of the group were particularly interested in exploring how insights from the sciences of complexity might enhance our ways of making sense of life in organizations. Even before my encounter with Oliveira I had been fascinated with questions around how innovation actually occurred. For some years I had worked in industry and found mainstream ways of thinking quite limited when it came to understanding how innovation came about and how it was blocked in my own work experience. My encounter with Oliveira only increased my interest and on beginning to read about the implications of the complexity sciences for understanding organizations, I came to sense a close link with my interest in innovation.

I found the discussions in the doctoral group very challenging. We all talked about chaos and complexity, at first using terms and concepts drawn from the natural sciences, without being at all clear about what they might mean in terms of human behaviour. We talked about various approaches to psychology and tried to make links, again without being all that clear about what we meant. Some of the group members were interested in social constructionism and began to make links between the construction of social realties in conversations (Shotter, 1993) and the emergence of order in complex systems. The focus of attention in our own conversations began to shift to the nature of human communicative interaction and how unpredictable its emergent patterns were.

As I write about this experience now, with the benefit of hindsight, it sounds as if we were pursuing an orderly path of inquiry. However, the experience at the time was quite different. Most of the time I found it difficult to understand what some of my colleagues were saying because they came from very different backgrounds to my own, both in terms of national cultures and in terms of professional disciplines. I know that others had this experience too and that many found it equally difficult to understand what I, with my Portuguese and "techno-economic" background, was talking about. Although we were all using the English language, it was as if we were talking in different languages. The whole process of searching together for some meaning in what we were talking about was certainly not orderly or efficient. Much of what we talked about seemed superfluous and unnecessary. There was much confusion with small interventions here and there leading us down conversational pathways that seemed to lead to dead ends. At times we became very irritated with each other and went home quite disappointed at seemingly having got nowhere or made sense of anything. I was struck by the degree of our misunderstanding of each other and at the lack of efficiency, the endless iteration and duplication of our conversational practice. However, after some time, I began to notice how the misunderstanding between us provoked even more determined efforts to formulate some kind of understanding. I also began to notice how the escalating misunderstanding between us sometimes seemed to provoke sudden breakthroughs into some insight that we had not previously had. I began to think that perhaps, after all, this inefficient process of going repetitively around the same points, this redundancy, each time revealing new sources of misunderstanding was the very process that generates new insight. And it became increasingly clear how this experience made sense in terms of, resonated with, insights from the complexity sciences. This, it seemed, was how the order of new meaning emerged in the disorder of misunderstanding and diversity.

Then it dawned on me that the process in our doctoral group mirrored Oliveira's experience. He too engaged in endless conversations over a number of years with colleagues in various settings. They too found it difficult to understand each other because they came from different professional backgrounds to talk about pipelines, ducts and galleries. From what I could gather, most of these conversations were redundantly diverse in the same sense as those in the doctoral group. They inefficiently repeated and duplicated previous conversations in the same group or conversations in other groups. They were also characterized by many small and large differences appearing to be random variations or fluctuation that might nevertheless escalate into new insights. Furthermore, the conversations they engaged in displayed the same process of misunderstanding provoking the search for new meaning as the one I encountered in the doctoral group. I began to think that innovation was essentially a conversational process, a process of communicative interaction between people characterized by redundant diversity experienced as misunderstanding, all of which seemed to be requirements for the emergence of novelty. It also became clear how this process of communicative interaction both formed and was formed by power relations and consequent feelings of inclusion and exclusion. Some people were initially far more versed in using the "new" language of complexity and this immediately conferred on them a more powerful presence in the conversation than others had. They became the included, the "in-group", while others felt excluded in the "out-group". Those in the "in-group" could terminate particular conversational themes with authoritative pronouncements and by so doing in effect keep the conversation stuck within a particular set of assumptions. Again the parallels with Oliveira's story are, for me, quite striking.

But what was it that kept us together and what was it that kept us going on talking in that doctoral group, despite feeling very frustrated and getting annoyed and irritated with each other? I think it was trust and the mutual expectation that together we could make more sense than we could do individually. It came to feel, for me anyway, that we were essential to each other in terms of what we were seeking to do. And of course, we not only became irritated with each other. I think we also greatly enjoyed being and working together. There was tension and excitement, pleasure and irritation, all at the same time. As we worked together, we began to make more sense to each other. The level of misunderstanding seemed to decline and our proceeding together seemed to become a great deal more orderly and efficient. We seemed to have developed a common language in our discussions that collapsed the potential misunderstanding. We felt that the words we were using were no longer triggering endless semantic discussions because we now "knew" what they "meant". We began to produce more or less coherent papers for discussion, which took on a more peaceful tone. To anyone entering the group at that stage, it might appear that we had all along been following a rather linear path of systematic, programmed search now embodied in our papers. Much of the redundant diversity and misunderstanding had largely dissipated and what was now evident was more or less coherent "products", which might hopefully be described as innovative. Except that, of course, the new entrant to the group, not possessing the language that had evolved in our interaction, would now, in reading the papers and in engaging in the discussions, experience misunderstanding again, as the precursor to developing new meaning. Once again, the parallels with Oliveira's story became clearer to me.

I think that the experience I have been describing in the doctoral group is in itself an example of what innovation is and how it emerges. The conversational diversity of people with different backgrounds, the redundant explorations and the misunderstanding generated were all ways of talking that were essential to the emergence of new themes and new sense. Again, I thought this was mirroring the interactions of Oliveira with others, in which his new products and processes emerged. Just as in the doctoral group, so in Oliveira's story it would be easy to lose sight of the long process characterized by redundant diversity and misunderstanding in which the final products had emerged. I began to think of an innovation as the materialization of new meaning that emerged in the messy, paradoxical process of communicative interaction outlined above.

The story of systems development at a water utility

As the understanding I have described above began to mature I continued to explore the practice of innovation. I knew the Director of Human Resources at Epal, a water utility in Lisbon, and I contacted him to see if there were any interesting projects I might become involved with in some way. He mentioned a digitized survey that was being developed and suggested that I make a formal request to the board, which would have to be backed by a formal letter from my doctoral supervisors. Fortunately, the President of the company was a former colleague of Professor João Caraça, one of these supervisors. I soon received permission and contacted the Director of Information Technology at Epal who was very accommodating, even though I had no formal plan of what I wanted to do. The easygoing attitude of the IT Director made it possible for me to wander around relevant departments and engage in both formal and less formal conversations. Over the period from 1995 to 1998, I spent a considerable amount of time talking to people from a number of levels in the hierarchy and from many different departments. I was interested in how the digitized survey my friend had mentioned constituted an innovation, how it had come about, and how it was evolving. I will start by recounting some of what I learned in my conversations with people about this organization's background and the beginnings of the innovation up to my arrival in 1995.

Epal's background

Epal is the state-owned supplier of water to Lisbon and surrounding areas. The possibility of privatization had been a matter of public discussion for some time and it was widely accepted that the monopoly in the water sector would eventually be broken up. Many feared that this would enable foreign entry into the industry; in order to prepare for this threat, Epal was investing in a substantial modernization of the distribution network.

Epal was organized into departments having the following functions:

- Production: capturing the water and transporting it to Lisbon.
- Treatment: making the water drinkable.
- Distribution: delivering the water to consumers.
- Consumer Relations: registering consumers, measuring consumption, invoicing, collecting payments and generally solving problems with households.
- Planning and construction of extensions to the distribution network.
- Maintenance and improvement of the distribution network.

The government appoints the members of the Epal board for three to four year periods and the majority of the members do not normally serve for more than one term. Since 1989, the company had undergone three significant changes in organizational structure recommended by consultants. However, these involved only limited compulsory redundancies and few changes in physical locations, tasks and workflow. Sometimes departments were reorganized but tasks and processes remained the same. On other occasions, departments were given new names, but people carried on doing what they had been doing before. The typical decision-making process at Epal takes the form of conversations between heads of department, in which they accommodate each other's expectations and interests in order to reach a compromise. A decision is then presented to the Board, which legitimizes it. Power lies with the heads of departments who have usually been in the company for long enough to understand its culture.

↳ decision-making process

That culture might be described as a culture of artisans, that is, one of learning by doing and being taught by artisans. This "craftsmanship" culture was expressed in a number of ways. For example, there was considerable peer pressure to do things "right" as opposed to doing things cheaply. Self-improvement was valued more than "doing things by the book". People mentioned pride in belonging to this company and sharing its technical culture and professional attitude. On several occasions, I took part in conversations between workers about corporate heroes from the past. They had become heroes because of their professional expertise and their ability to improvise good technical solutions to difficult problems. Older employees transmitted to younger colleagues a sense of belonging and pride in being members of a company reputed for its technical expertise and improvisational flexibility. People were interested in new ways of doing things and in new materials. Indeed, technical processes had been changing markedly over the past ten years. These changes, mainly to do with automation, were initiated and developed from within the company, with the cooperation of consultants and suppliers. However, because of such technological innovation, the company was moving from its culture of "craftsmanship" to one of disciplined scientific knowledge. This meant moving from a company that possessed an elite of artisan workers to an engineering company. This move was, in turn, altering perceptions of the value and status of various departments within the company. It was also altering patterns of conversation.

Note how I have been describing the kind of culture that those taking the entrepreneurial/social perspective on innovation would approve of. However, as far as I can tell, no charismatic leader had put them there. I heard no talk about visions. This culture, understood as habitual themes organizing the experience of being together, had emerged in the long history of interaction between people in this organization. And the very interaction in these habitual terms was transforming itself in ways that might become less amenable to innovation. Again, however, no leader was putting the change there and no one was designing new values or realizing some kind of prior vision.

evolved as a result of interaction b/w people in the organization

Within the context I have just outlined, I was interested in an innovation that had to do with repairs to the water distribution system.

Repairs to the water distribution system

A number of people explained to me what the procedure was that led to repairs being made to the distribution system. Customers would telephone to report leaks in the street or interruptions to the supply of water to their premises. The sequence of communications their calls triggered is depicted in Figure 4.1.

The Customer Service department received the call and passed the information to the Operations Department (OD). An inspector travelled to the location and assessed the problem. In order to make an assessment he needed an updated map of the area and a survey of its underground pipe network. This enabled him to identify which valves should be closed in order to stop the flooding. He notified OD, where priorities were set and an order for repair issued and sent to the Maintenance Department. Typically within the day, a crew left the nearest company site to repair the leaking pipes. This crew also needed charts containing updated records of the type and dimension of pipes in place. On completion of the repair, a report was prepared on the work done, recording components replaced, type of materials used, and the nature of the damage to the failed components. The reports were used to update the charts of the network.

On average, there were more than 300 repairs of this kind each day and the drawing room could not cope with the flow of information. The charts therefore tended to be updated on a piecemeal basis so that several versions of the same charts existed at any one time. People responded to the consequent unreliability of the charts by keeping their own private databases with different ways of recording and retrieving data. Unbeknown to senior managers, these private databases had proliferated throughout the company. People reached for whatever was to hand (computers, paper cards, sheets of paper, recording books, writing directly on their charts) to store the information that they expected to need in the near future.

Note here how people were interacting in local situations in the living present in order to use the procedural and information tools that they had available to them. Note also how that interaction takes the form of conversation.

However, this way of dealing with the information people required to do their work gave rise to a number of problems:

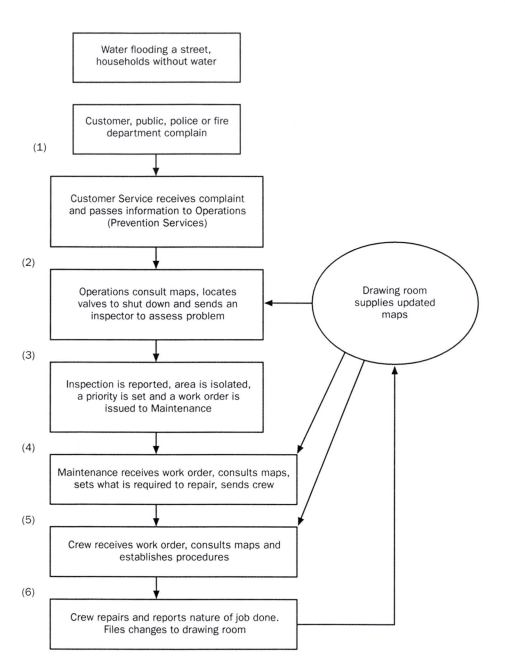

Figure 4.1 *The flow of information in EPAL*

- Customer Service did not know when a complaint related to a problem already reported and so passed duplicate information to Operations. Customer Service staff had no way of knowing what was being done further down the line and so could not answer customer inquiries about how their complaints were being handled.
- Under the pressure of work in peak periods, two or more inspectors might be sent to address the same problem.
- Since charts might not yet have been updated, they may well not have recorded the most recent components installed on site.
- Even when charts had actually been updated, confidence was so low that people did not believe that they had been updated and so checked up on what the charts showed by talking to others and so gaining access to their personal information systems. Each service organized its own set of charts (thirty-eight covering the city area) and believed that their own charts were more likely to reflect what was actually under the ground.
- Crews often had to contact the office to obtain more up-to-date information on the site they were working on.

The result was the daily production of huge quantities of data, much of which was duplicated and stored in ways that were incompatible with each other. Many people talked about how useful it would be if this data were recorded and disseminated in real time. Those operating the pipeline system would then be able to function much more efficiently. So over the years there had been conversations about digitizing the surveys of the pipe network and storing these surveys on computer where they could be accessed at work sites. In this way, the most up-to-date information could be accessed and any change made to the network could be immediately recorded electronically onto the digitized charts.

Developing a digitalized cartographic system

In 1989, the head of the Distribution Department decided to pursue the idea of developing a digitized survey of the network. However, the departmental budget could not accommodate the significant cost of the technology and labour that would be required for this endeavour. Furthermore, he knew that this issue was not, at that time, a major concern of the Board. Their investment priority was the development of the distribution network. So, he set in motion a less ambitious project within the department, using internal resources without formal approval.

Two new engineers were hired and, although their roles had nothing formally to do with the digitization project, they were chosen because they had skills relevant to it. Soon, they were spending most of their time on the digitized survey. Later, in spite of financial constraints, a consultant was appointed to assist on the project. During this phase, the development of the project depended on the motivation and effort of four people. Although their actions had not been legitimized, they were tolerated in a culture that emphasized technical progress and technical expertise.

Note how these events are quite consistent with the entrepreneurial/ social explanation of innovation. A need has been identified and a champion appears who goes around the legitimate procedures in a culture that enables such conduct. All that is lacking is the kind of supportive leader emphasized in the entrepreneurial/social perspective.

This first phase of the project consisted mainly of the digitization of the existing maps of Lisbon. However, existing charts were drawn to different scales and this made it difficult for people to move from one chart to the next. Clearly, this would not do for an instrument that was supposed to be used as a tool for rapid identification of which pipeline branches to shut down. All charts, therefore, would not only have to be digitized but also reduced to a common scale if the system was to work. The routine work of loading the information was subcontracted to a consultant who placed people in-house to work under the supervision of a team leader from Epal. It was intended that in this phase the work should be conducted in two shifts using two digitization tables. However, the cooperation of other departments required for this was never obtained and therefore a smaller group of people carried on loading and monitoring the quality of the work being done. Because of resource constraints, the work had to be done on a small PC which could not provide the processing speed and memory required for a digitized survey.

The task was becoming impossible. Each day, charts were being changed as much as they were being digitized, so that catching up with the changes became a vicious cycle. This went on until 1994.

Despite its apparent failure, however, this first attempt was very important in drawing attention to the survey and in establishing a general agreement on the need for such a system. During this period, "know-how" was developed on the way such processes could be carried out and what requirements and difficulties this entailed. Agreement was also reached on the symbols to be used so that all who needed to refer to them could understand the maps. Most importantly, these initial efforts were developing within Epal the skills required to digitize geographical information systems, a technology that had so far only been developed by the military. Epal was, therefore, a pioneer in Portugal in this field. During 1990/91 Lisbon's local government heard about this work and expressed interest in acquiring the digitized maps in order to more effectively control other companies who were burying structures beneath city soil. However, this had the consequence of slowing down the development of the digitization project, because the project manager was required to attend many city council commissions addressing the survey issue, none of which produced anything concrete. However, the reputation Epal was developing in this area was to become one of the foundations of a number of strategic moves that the company is now making in international markets. It was used as a basis for a bid that Epal made for work in Brazil.

Notice here the emergence of unexpected opportunities, all in the absence of any kind of vision or plan.

By 1995, when I first began to talk to people about this innovation, the product concept of digitized charts was in the process of being revised. It was beginning to be redefined as a wider information system and it was decided that a database function should be included. I was very interested in how this redefinition was taking place.

① product concept
② redefinition
③ database.

Revision of the concept

As far as I could tell, the main reason for the redefinition was that the project moved from the Distribution Department to the Information Technology (IT) Department. The move took place because the head of the Distribution Department was promoted to another area and the head of the IT department became interested in speeding the process up because it fitted in with what he was already doing. The IT department already possessed some knowledge of digitized surveys since they had been developing such a system for the large pipeline coming from the dams in north of the country, internally known as the production system.

The digitization work done in OD was taken over by staff in IT who used a UNIX platform and more powerful programming tools. They also had consulting expertise in geographic systems and graph technology. Naturally, given who was now developing it, the project was redefined as an information technology project and coupled with the other project that was then underway for the production system. The project was no longer simply to develop a digitized survey of the distribution network to assist engineers in carrying out repairs. It was now a project to develop a more dynamic total information system. Therefore, relational database programming was introduced. In 1995, there was another shift in the platform used to develop the project, which changed from a non-Windows platform to a Windows NT environment.

What I particularly noticed here was the shift in the nature of the conversations about digitized surveys. The dominant conversation of mechanical engineers was yielding to other conversations that were acquiring greater legitimacy. The vocabulary and the concepts in these new conversations were coming from information sciences, biology, management sciences and organizational psychology.

The years that followed this move saw a growing consensus on the importance of the project. It became more and more public, receiving official recognition. This improved its priority in the investment programme, resulting in an increased budget. By the end of 1995, all cartographic data (names of streets, topographic heights) were introduced into the databases, but up-to-date information about technical data, such as pipe dimensions and type of material, valves and faucets, was still absent. The early maps that had been digitized were not being updated. Another six months were spent trying to bring the system into line with current changes in the materials installed in the ground. By mid-1996, other departments were brought in to contribute to the improvement of the system. It was at this stage that several unofficial databases came to light.

The pilot survey was ready for testing in October 1996 and a dialogue began with user departments. Several technical issues emerged during this dialogue and were addressed. Furthermore, participating in the dialogue made the system less threatening to people. In the last quarter of 1996 the first of a number of programmes took place to train people in how to use the new system. Three workstations were placed in each department that had to use the system, namely, Customer Services, Operations and Maintenance. People were invited to "play" and comment on the use of the system. They were asked to absorb their "private" databases into the new system. People in technical sections appeared to be willing to cooperate since it meant official recognition and appreciation of the activities they had engaged in for years.

I was interested in how people had developed their own databases in order to overcome the inadequacies of the formal information systems. They had done so over the years in conversations that were quite unknown to those higher up in the hierarchy. The existence of these private databases came as a surprise during the programmes to train people to use the new system. The informal databases now began to affect the design of the new system. For example, new entry fields in the databases of the new system were added. It became clear that contextual information about the precise site conditions in which repairs would have to be conducted in different locations could not be depicted on the charts. They could not depict, for instance, that cars were parked in a particular street in such a way as to obstruct the work. This was usually dealt with by workers going into nearby cafes to ask whom the car belonged to and request its removal. This took less time than the prescribed, formal procedure of summoning the police. For me, the interesting point was how the digitized survey had been able to absorb the narrative knowledge that had emerged from within the departments. In other words, the innovation "absorbed" previous "unrecorded" innovations that were the emergent result of people's conversations about the way they could simplify their lives or about how they could solve practical problems they faced in their day-to-day activities.

People on the training courses welcomed the new system. Indeed they were so enthusiastic that they began to complain about the quality and speed of the computers they had been given to learn from. They also began to complain about a lack of commitment to the new system on the part of upper management. There did seem to be a lack of decisive direction on the part of upper levels in management. Budgets for the required number of computers and plotters were still not confirmed by February 1997. However, an extensive training programme was approved and the person who had been working in the project since 1994 trained more than 30 future operators.

complaints from trainees?

One interesting consequence of the training programmes was the expectations to which they gave rise. Operators were expecting the digitized system to be immediately usable in a perfect state. They complained that the survey would never be perfect enough because it would never be up to date with current realities on sites. It appears that when it came to the operational phase, they forget the lessons from the development phase, where there were many surprises as the process unfolded. People seemed to forget the fact that the charts had never been up to date and required them to improvise. Now they demanded that the survey be absolutely foolproof if they were to use it. They seem to have lost sight of the fact that if they did not operate with the system in its current state and so feed it with updates, it would never be updated, just as the charts never were. It seemed that they were coming to believe that systems could completely replace improvisation.

I would like to comment on this development because I think it reflects an important point. If one thinks of human action as a system then it is the system that should be doing the work. But systems are tools in a wider process of communicative interaction. The danger of mistaking the tool for the interaction is that it distracts attention from the wider process and the impact that tools have on this wider process. This should become more evident as the story proceeds.

[handwritten margin note: systems are just tools]

Further evolution

The digitized survey system was a horizontal process running through nearly all departments. It was perceived as a new "power tool", which might enable those who created and managed it to threaten the status of others. The main issue seemed to relate to career progression. Mechanical engineering graduates used to expect to climb the corporate ladder, while other people had more limited career expectations. However, in recent years the main pattern of talk had shifted from the vocabulary and concepts of mechanical engineers to those of computer scientists. This change in patterns of talk was shifting patterns of power and status; the digitized survey system powerfully symbolized this shift.

During the training sessions, there were many discussions on how the survey should operate, what kind of information it should store and how it would be retrieved. These discussions led the sector leaders to suggest the use of the survey for transmission of information about work and repair orders. By January 1997, the system was reconfigured and a new function was introduced. The communications between departments regarding work orders would be done through the survey. The survey would no longer simply be an information platform but would become a control system as well. This notion led to the installation of flow-of-work procedures.

In the new system, a repair order was to be processed in the following way:

1 Opening: receiving information of disruption to distribution.
2 Inspection: Operations send someone to assess the problem.

3 Execution: issuing a work order and passing it to Maintenance.
4 Closing: doing the work and filing a report on the system.

It was not possible to alter the information as it passed from one step to another. The computer automatically registered the time of recording and expedition of this information. Costs of repair, materials used and recovered, and labour costs were all stored in this system for each work order. If the President of the company wished, he could see which repairs were being done and so could anyone else in the company, provided that they could access the system. This would be very easy because workstations were to be located in all the departments.

The digital survey was, therefore, clearly changing from simply being a tool that increased efficiency to an instrument of control and performance evaluation. Since the system identified the time when a communication took place, it could be used to analyse time differentials between issuing the order and completing the repair. In addition, it identified who sent, received and issued communications. This was no longer a geographic information system but now a process control system.

The importance of shifting power relations in the process of innovation is particularly striking here. It is also noteworthy how the use of tools of communication affects power relations, hence the importance of focusing attention not just on the tools but also on what part they play in wider processes of human relating.

One of the most interesting aspects of this story for me, as I took part in conversations about it between 1995 and 1998, was the way in which it changed its nature. As the conversations about it evolved, as changes in the context were occurring (technologies, organizational structures, technological updating of processes) the project was being reconfigured and redefined. It started as a faster process of updating information. It moved to a horizontal information sharing platform. It became an efficient problem solving system. It moved to an operational information support system. Finally, it was defined as a part of an integrated information management system that is really an on-line device for management control. The curious thing is that the system itself was even then not yet in full operation.

This project started as a tentative, limited and located process. It then moved into a traditional top-down re-engineering process comprising a clear purpose, a detailed budget and a detailed phase schedule. However, a much more messy and emergent development process was really changing the outcomes and the meanings of this innovation. The more formal approach to the process did not envisage, for instance, that the innovation would accommodate previous innovative actions developed by those who had simply responded to the problems they faced every day.

In this story of innovation, one can find aspects of both the rational planning and the entrepreneurial/social perspectives on innovation. However, I am suggesting that they are simply aspects of much wider processes of complex responsive relating between people. In the sections that follow, I want to explore some of the key features of complex responsive processes of relating to which this story points.

The absence of the heroic entrepreneur

Unlike Oliveira's story in Chapter 2, there is no corporate hero or central individual in the innovation processes described in this chapter. Instead there were various people at various times interacting with each other and it was in their interaction that the innovation emerged. Nearly everyone who worked during the first phase had gone by the time of the last reported phase. During the process, a split in the consulting company occurred and the new company devoted its resources mainly to the project. During this period Epal went through three major restructuring phases. Project leadership changed. Technologies were adopted and abandoned. Programming tools were replaced by later versions. As far as the planning of the process is concerned, scheduled milestones reflected more the political and cultural processes of the innovation development than the schedule of work activities and its logical sequences.

The innovation had no clear "champion" or someone who could easily be identified in the company as the survey promoter. There was no continuing support for the innovation from the top of the hierarchy. However, we might understand why this innovation survived despite the absence of clear support from the top for a long time, if we regard it as the result of a powerful and meaningful stream of conversations. These conversations emerged in local situations, spreading from one local situation to another. We might also understand why the innovation turned out to be very different to what was expected at the beginning, if we pay attention to shifting conversational patterns. The conditions of birth of this innovation illustrate what I mean by dissipation in social settings. The initial work done on the digitized survey was not official. It was simply tolerated because people at the top trusted the director who was

role of mistakes

promoting this bootleg activity. A number of people engaged in speculating about what the survey could be and started working tentatively. A number of steps were taken and learning occurred. There was no clear form of appraising the added value of what these people were talking about before they embarked on their actions. Their words and their actions could be regarded as redundant because a large number of "mistakes" were made. However, the classification of those actions as mistakes is easy to make today because we now know that back at the start, the capacity of the computers they used was not sufficient, the development tools were not adequate and the symbols used were not good enough. Nevertheless, those mistakes were instrumental in the acquisition of experience in a new technology (geographic systems) and in the assessment of the problems that would have to be dealt with.

The story told in this chapter points to aspects normally missing in the descriptions of innovation processes. Descriptions of innovations normally start at the point at which it is possible to set out a project with scheduled activities and milestones. This starting point omits the redundant, dissipative activities that create the historical context of an innovation's origins and influence its direction.

Power relations

The innovation was framed by the internal political dynamics and at the same time, it served as a vehicle for the expression of the political debate. That is, the innovation emerged as a product of conflicting interests while at the same time forming and potentially transforming those interests. The system moved from a more effective way of handling information to a centralization of information scattered across the company, then to a communication system and now to a control system. However, when the project is discussed these issues do not surface. Political interests or personal expectations, without consideration or judgement for how legitimate these might be, are concealed in rational debates. The words used refer to the degree of speed, reliability, effectiveness and improved efficiency. The promoters of the innovation argue about the "logical" nature and self-evident benefits of the process. Those who have, or feel they have something to lose from the system, emphasize the prudence one must adopt with regard to such "revolutionary systems" and cast doubts on the efficiency of the process; or they simply point to how the system is not being updated.

What is not brought into the open is the fear that expertise in areas likely to grow in importance is being accumulated in the department developing the innovation. This department is then put at the centre of developments likely to shape the future of the whole company. The survey will affect the tasks of many workers, although it will not entail any lay-offs. However, the department primarily responsible for developing the system will manage it and this is leading to concern in other departments about shifts in the balance of power.

Conclusion

This story illustrates how a self-organizing process of conversation displaying a critical level of misunderstanding simultaneously originated in, and subverted, a more stable and predictable innovation process. It also illustrates how emergent meanings can constitute the basis for new streams of talk that might change the official patterns of talk.

5 Innovation as complex responsive processes

- The complexity sciences as source domain for analogies with human interaction
- Interpreting the analogies in terms of human action
- Differences between mainstream thinking and the perspective of complex responsive processes
- What organizations are
- How innovation arises
- What innovation is
- Conclusion

In Chapter 2, I pointed to two rather different ways in which innovation is understood in mainstream management thinking. From the first perspective, innovations originate in the minds of reasoning individuals who identify unsatisfied market and organizational needs, set goals for the innovation and then deduce how they might be met. The process of realizing the innovation goals is governed by self-regulating planning systems. From the second perspective, innovations originate in the minds of intuitive, creative, heroic individual entrepreneurs and product champions. The process of realizing the innovation is governed by political and cultural systems, and those systems conducive to innovation are characterized by particular kinds of values or beliefs, and by particular kinds of visionary, charismatic leadership.

In Chapters 3 and 4, I described and reflected upon two experiences of innovation and suggested that mainstream ways of thinking, that is, either or both of the perspectives mentioned above, provide only limited ways of making sense of these experiences. I suggested that this limitation arises because the processes of innovation in practice are essentially participative experiences of direct interaction between people, most significantly taking the form of conversation. Neither strand of mainstream thinking accords central importance to such direct participative conversational interaction. To the extent that they deal with the social at all, mainstream perspectives do so from an understanding that individuals are parts participating in a social system. The notion here is one of participation as taking part in a wider system, whereas my interpretation of participation in the innovation experiences is of people interacting directly with each other.

In this chapter, I will be developing what I mean by this distinction between direct participation and the notion of participating in a system. As a result, I think, of their systemic notions of participation, both strands of mainstream thinking, in their different ways, do not focus attention on the kinds of inefficient, messy interaction in which innovations emerge in shifting patterns of power relations and accompanying dynamics of inclusion and exclusion.

what mainstream thinking missed?

In this chapter, I want to review a way of thinking that does focus attention on the experience of human interaction, understood as the experience of direct participation. This is the theory of complex responsive processes developed in earlier volumes in the series of which this book is one (Stacey, 2001; Stacey *et al.*, 2000). This theory draws on analogies from the complexity sciences, interpreting those analogies in terms of relationship psychology (Stacey, 2000). The theory is developed in some detail in the publications mentioned, so in this chapter I will give only a brief summary, paying particular attention to the link with innovation. I will first point to some key insights from the sciences of complexity and the analogies they provide for human action. I will then summarize how they might be interpreted in terms of organizations, when understood from the perspective of relationship psychology. The rest of the chapter will develop those aspects of the theory of complex responsive processes that seem to me to have most to do with innovation.

The complexity sciences as source domain for analogies with human interaction

Those taking a complexity perspective in the natural sciences adopt the standard position of the objective observer and think of natural phenomena in terms of systems consisting typically of vast numbers of interacting entities. The focus of their attention is on the interaction between entities. They understand this interaction in terms of continuous nonlinear iteration or reproduction, in which the immediate past is reproduced in the present, which will be reproduced in the future. Perhaps the key question complexity scientists deal with is how, in the absence of any kind of programme or blueprint, such interaction between enormous numbers of entities produces the order, pattern or coherence that can be observed. For example, how do orderly organic structures arise in the interaction of the enormous numbers of genes in the genome of species? Or how do coherent patterns of evolution occur in the interaction between enormous numbers of species? Or how do patterns of thought arise in the interactions of enormous numbers of neurons and chemicals in the human brain? Or, how do consistent patterns of physical and chemical activity arise in the interactions between enormous numbers of molecules?

In general, in answer to such questions, natural complexity scientists explore particular versions of a general hypothesis. This is that the global pattern, coherence or order in all of these phenomena and many others, emerges in the local, self-organizing interaction of the entities. They set out to show how it is quite possible that self organization, understood as local interaction in the complete absence of any blueprint or plan, can produce emergent global pattern. In different ways they all show how particular kinds of dynamic arise when interaction has particular characteristics of diversity and of connectivity, which both enable and constrain interaction between identities. Some have called this particular kind of dynamic "the edge of chaos" and demonstrate how it is a paradoxical pattern of change that is both stable and unstable at the same time. In this particular kind of dynamic very small changes can escalate into altered global pattern. In others words, transformative change occurs though the amplification of small differences. Some complexity scientists show how, in these particular kinds of dynamic, it is quite possible for both continuity and potential transformation to emerge at the same time. In other words, they show how novelty, creativity or innovation can emerge in interaction. A widely used method is computer simulation, which demonstrates the possibility of the above hypothesis in the medium of digital symbols.

There is more than one complexity science and there is more than one way of understanding their implications. Stacey, Griffin and Shaw (2000) have provided a detailed overview of these different strands and ways of thinking. I therefore will say no more on the matter, other than to indicate that I will be drawing on the particular form of complexity thinking that they identify as the basis of complex responsive process theory. This is a way of thinking about complex systems as interaction between diverse entities that amplifies difference to produce emergent novelty. The causal framework here is that which Stacey, Griffin and Shaw have identified as Transformative Teleology, a way of thinking in which the future is

various types of teleology

understood to be under perpetual construction. This is in contrast to the other kinds of teleological framework identified in Chapter 2. Natural Law Teleology understands the future to be a repetition of the past according to natural laws. Formative Teleology understands the future to be the unfolding of what is already enfolded in the past and present. Neither framework can, therefore, explain the emergence of novelty. Adaptionist Teleology explains the emergence of novelty through the operation of natural selection on chance variation at the level of entities. Transformative Teleology, however, explains the emergence of novelty in terms of local self-organizing interaction between entities in the present. I will draw on the strand of complexity thinking in the natural sciences that Stacey, Griffin and Shaw have argued is consistent with Transformative Teleology.

Interpreting the analogies in terms of human action

The theory of complex responsive processes (Stacey 2001; Stacey *et al.*, 2000) draws on the natural complexity sciences as a source domain of analogies with human action. The basic analogy is provided by interaction. Although the complexity sciences utilize systems as a way of thinking, the theory of complex responsive processes is not a systems theory. On the contrary, it is based on the argument that it is highly limiting, and in the end inappropriate, to think of human interaction as a system. I will not go into that argument here because it is well rehearsed in the references I have given. The theory of complex responsive process is a process theory; a theory of the process of interaction understood as paradoxical, as dialectical. The abstract nature of interaction in the complexity sciences is interpreted in human terms on the basis of the thought of the sociologist George Herbert Mead (1934).

For Mead, the basic unit of analysis in human action was the social act consisting of the gesture of one person to another, which calls forth a response in the gesturer that is similar to the response called forth in the other. The meaning of interaction for both parties arises in this social act. Meaning cannot be located in either the gesture or the response phase of what is one act. The capacity for one's gesture to call forth the same response in oneself as in another gives rise to significant symbols. The significant symbol is the response called forth in oneself that is similar to the response called forth in another. The basis of communication, therefore, is significant symbols, that is, actions of a body. Because of this capacity to form symbols human beings can know; they can think. Thinking, the mind, is a private role play, a silent conversation of the body with itself, just as the social is public role play, a vocal conversation of bodies with each other. In this sense the individual mind and the social are one and the same phenomenon, at the same level of analysis. The basis of human action of any kind is thus communicative interaction in the medium of symbols. And this communicative interaction has the same properties of interaction between entities as understood in the complexity sciences. In other words, the dynamics of human communicative interaction can also be understood in terms of enabling constraints and diversity in which much the same patterns of continuity and potential transformation emerge. Human interaction patterns itself in self-organizing ways. Human interaction is self organization in the local situations of the living present and it is in such interaction that human futures are perpetually constructed. Indeed it is how human individual and social identities are perpetually constructed.

In the theory of complex responsive process, human communicative interaction is basically a conversational process comprising not just the symbols of language but also the bodily rhythms of communicating people, that is the symbols of emotion. Communicative interaction forms and is formed by emergent themes. Central to this perspective, then, is the notion that experience is interaction and it is patterned in narrative and propositional themes to do with being together. These conversational themes are continually reproduced as habits and variations on those habits. The dynamics are such that variations are always potentially transformed into new habits. While such interaction cannot be thought of as a system, in their communicative interaction people do design systems, which they use as tools in that communicative interaction.

Interaction is patterned as enabling constraints and in human terms this is what power means. So, central to the theory of complex responsive responses is the notion that all human communicative interaction is inevitably patterned as power relations. Drawing on the work of the sociologist Norbert Elias (1939, 1970, 1989; Elias and Scotson, 1994), these figurations of power relations reflect ideological themes organizing the experience of being together and they are always reflected in the dynamics of inclusion and exclusion.

I will be elaborating on and developing some of the notions presented in the above highly condensed description of the theory of complex responsive processes in the sections that follow, insofar as they are relevant to the perspective I take on innovation. However, before I do that it might be helpful to summarize the difference between the complex responsive process perspective and those of mainstream thinking about innovation.

Differences between mainstream thinking and the perspective of complex responsive processes

mainstream Thinking

Both strands in mainstream thinking explain the origin, formation, cause and evolution of innovation in terms of constructs outside the ordinary experience of interaction between people in the living present of local situations. They do this in a "both ... and" manner of thinking to argue that innovations are formed in *both*:

- the mind of the autonomous individual, who is understood as a rational calculating being in the rational planning school and an intuitive, political, heroic being in the entrepreneurial school

and

- a system understood as a self-regulating control system in the rational planning school and as a cultural, vision-driven system in the entrepreneurial school.

CRP

The theory of complex responsive processes differs in that it explains the origins, formation, cause and evolution of novelty and innovation in terms of interaction itself. Drawing on analogies from the complexity sciences, the fundamental argument is that iterative nonlinear interaction in the medium of symbols itself has inherent pattern forming properties, making it unnecessary to posit causal constructs outside of the process of interaction. Interactions between entities that are connected and diverse enough have the inherent capacity to generate repetitive and novel emergent patterns at the same time. This happens because complex nonlinear interaction simultaneously constrains, or dampens, difference and amplifies it. What we can say is that coherence, or pattern, will emerge in nonlinear interaction, provided that connectivity and diversity are not too great, but that there is no guarantee such coherence will be good or even successful. Judgements of good or bad, success or failure, are made by humans as they experience the emergent patterns. By analogy, nonlinear interaction in the medium of symbols between human beings will have the same intrinsic pattern forming properties. This means that there is no system or autonomous individual outside the interaction that can be said to be causing or forming the interaction. Persons form and are formed by interaction so that the notion of an autonomous individual is simply an abstraction from experience, a conceptual device. What we call culture is not a system outside interaction but themes emerging in interaction that are characterized by a high degree of repetitiveness with little variation; in other words, habits. Control is not exercised by persons submitting to a system. Rather, control is inherent in interaction. It is because interaction both constrains and enables that it displays coherence or control. The control is inherent in the process, not in a system or an individual standing outside the interaction. The theory of complex responsive process moves from "both ... and" thinking that eliminates paradox to a paradoxical, dialectical way of thinking.

Taking this perspective means seeking to explain innovation from within my interaction with those involved in the innovation. I listen to the stories of those involved, thereby interacting with them, as they recount the history of their interactions with others.

What organizations are

In both the rational planning and entrepreneurial/social theories of innovation reviewed in Chapter 2, "the organization" is basically assumed to be a system. In the first case the system is a designed self-regulating control system and in the second it is a designed functional/cultural system; in both cases the organization as a system is understood to consist of a set of activities conducted in order to attain specific goals. "The organization" is a reification abstracted from the human experience of interaction. In both of these theories, individual human agents are understood in "both ... and" terms in that they are both parts of the organizational system and autonomous individuals standing outside it and designing it. When the human agents are thought of as parts of the system, they are governed by the rules of the system and their actions unfold the enfolded design of the system. It follows that in their role as parts they are not autonomous and innovation, in the sense of the completely new, cannot arise in the system itself because its behaviour is the unfolding of what has already been enfolded in its design. On the other hand, when human agents are conceptualized in the other way as autonomous individuals standing outside the system, designing it and setting its goals, the origin of novelty is located in either the reasoning or intuitive mental processes of individuals. The teleological assumptions underlying this mainstream thinking have been mentioned in Chapter 2 and are explored in some detail in the first volume of this series (Stacey *et al.*, 2000).

From a complex responsive process perspective, what we perceive as organizations are temporary stabilizations of themes, that is, habits, organizing the experience of being together that emerge in the process of human interaction in local situations in the living present. Organizations, then, are iterative processes of communicative interaction, that is, repetitive patterns of human experience of being together in the living present, in which themes are continually reproduced, always with the potential for transformation. This potential lies in the possibility that small differences, variations in the reproduction of habits, will be amplified into new action with new meaning. This continual interaction between humans who are all forming intentions, choosing and acting in relation to each other as they go about their daily work together, both stabilizes around coherent, repetitive patterns of communicative interaction, and at the same time these patterns are potentially transformed by those same interactions. In a sense, systems thinking involves "extracting" the habitual patterns out of the process of their formation and continuous transformation and naming them as a system. This way of thinking tends to overlook the process in which the habitual patterns come to be what they are and how they are potentially undergoing emergent change in the local interactions between people in the living present. The assumption is made that it is possible for someone to step outside of their interaction and objectify the patterns of interaction "as if" they were an "it" and the "as if" reification is then overlooked. It is assumed that the whole system can be designed and controlled. From the perspective of complex responsive processes, no one can actually do this and so no one can arrange or operate on organizational processes of interaction, only participate in them. Instead of understanding "the organization" as the "tool" humans design and use, the complex responsive process perspective understands organizations to be local processes of communicative interaction in the living present in which people use any systems they might design as tools for communicating and acting jointly together in various ways.

The stories of innovating concrete pipes and digitized surveys recounted in the previous two chapters illustrate the processes I have been describing. Oliveira did not design some overall organizational system. What he was doing, I suggest, was participating in one conversation after another in which both the continuity and the transformation of his project emerged at the same time. Much the same can be said about the development of the digitized survey. This too was a story about participative interaction between many people over a long time period in which the form of the innovation emerged. It was continually reproduced as continuity and transformation as it moved from a survey to a control system.

The perspective I take, then, is one in which what we call "the organization" is temporarily "successful" patterns of interactions that participants accept as "good enough" to be continually repeated, so becoming organizational habits. This repetition constitutes the stability of collective identity, or organizational culture, which is habitual patterns of themes organizing the experience of being together. These themes are expressed in a particular "organizational language", that is, particular ways of talking together formed by participants at the same time as that language is forming their collective identity as well as aspects of their individual identities. This is the move away from the "both … and" thinking of systems perspectives to the paradoxical way of thinking of complex responsive processes. The repetition of "good enough" organizational habits (culture or language) increases efficiency in that people get better and better at what they are doing as they repeat it in a very similar way. These habitual ways of talking are patterned as legitimate themes organizing the experience of being together, reflecting what has emerged as the official ideology, which makes current figurations of power relations feel natural. Newcomers to "the organization" find that they must use the legitimate ways of talking if they are to be included.

Mainstream thinking tends to identify "the organization" with these repetitive patterns of language and power and then ignore the complex responsive process in which such "order" has emerged and in which it is potentially transformed. These repetitive patterns tend to be named and reified, using the legitimate language of the organization as if it were a system already existing outside of communicational processes. Within organizations themselves, people tend to reify already emerged habits, regarding them as "things" that have "always been there". This process of reification reduces perceived uncertainty and so lowers anxiety. It follows that people in organizations become used to the stability and security of habitual ways of talking and will feel threatened, even aggressive, when new ways of talking are introduced by someone. In the context of organizational life, people are not primarily and intentionally seeking novelty. Innovation does not emerge for its own sake. Even when powerful people perceive a need to think and talk in new ways for their organization to survive, there will always be defensive responses to deal with the anxiety that uncertainty arouses. Others will contest attempts to introduce new themes into formal, legitimate conversations and will try to deny the need for such conversations: "we have been doing this for the last twenty years and it has always worked before …". This tendency is understandable and inevitable not only as a defense against anxiety but also as an attempt to sustain existing power relations. When patterns of talking change, patterns of inclusion and exclusion change too and with them power relations are inevitably reconfigured. From the complex responsive process perspective, which takes human tendencies to defend themselves against anxiety and to sustain existing power relations as central, it becomes hopelessly naïve to believe that there could ever be a "culture" in which people benignly valued different ways of talking and loved innovation and change. This is because change threatens identities.

The points I am making about power relations, inclusion/exclusion and identity are all evident in the stories of drainage pipes and digitized survey told in the last two chapters. Oliveira's story is one of shifting power relations in his interactions with the banks, the cement companies and maintenance subcontractors. His development of novel pipe shapes and novel ways of manufacturing them all threatened the interests of the cement companies and the subcontractors. They implied a shift in power relations and thus some kind of transformation in the identities of those whose power was threatened. Their responses to the threat had a major impact on the evolution of Oliveira's innovations. At the water utility too, it is clear how the development of the digitized survey shifted power relations between departments. It is also clear how an underlying ideology of control made it feel natural for power relations to shift from engineers to information technologists. Such shifts in power relations were an integral part of the transformation of the innovation's meaning.

However, if people naturally tend to stabilize power relations and routines of communication and action, if they naturally tend to resist the introduction of new themes into their conversations, how and why do they produce new meaning? The problem becomes one of explaining how novelty arises. If innovation cannot be understood simply in terms of autonomous individuals of either the rational or heroic kind, then how is one to understand it? If the innovation process is not the operation of formal mechanisms of control or the product of a long political battle of elite entrepreneurs with visions of the future, then how is it to be understood?

From the perspective of complex responsive processes, the process of communicative interaction, in which habitual patterns are continually reproduced, is at the same time the process in which even small variations in the reproduction of habits are potentially amplified. The possibility of the emergent new lies in the inherent property of nonlinear interaction to amplify small differences. The origins of novelty and innovation therefore lie in differences. Innovation emerges in the amplification of the diversity between participants in interactive communication, even when that diversity is quite small. The processes that pattern our experience of being together are also the processes in which emerges the potential transformation of the pattern. We do not then think of an organization as something finished and complete that has to be changed by some external operation to something new. Instead we think of iterative communicative interactions in which both habits and potentially amplified variations around them are paradoxically emerging at the same time. In this way of thinking no organization is fixed but is always potentially changing in its perpetual reproduction. And if it does not change then this must be because communicative interaction is continually reproduced with very little variation and as themes that damp rather than amplify what little variation there is. In understanding why and how an organization is, or is not, changing, attention is focused on the way people are reproducing themes organizing their experience in their conversational life and what it is about such themes that amplify or damp difference. Attention is focused not on sharing and conforming to common cultures but on how in their participation people are spontaneously disturbing them with the consequence of increased diversity.

Again, the stories of the last two chapters illustrate the points I am making. Oliveira's story can be understood as a process of amplifying many small differences. For example, his response to the flood damage was different to that of others and because he happened to be reading about Roman drainage systems he developed a theme organizing his conversation with others to do with drainpipe shape. This was amplified in many conversations in very different communities. In his conversations and his other activities he was disturbing habitual ways of thinking and in doing so shifting power relations. The story of the digitized survey at the water utility is also one in which different ways of dealing with the problem of information about underground pipes were amplified in various ways over a number of years, culminating in a new management control system. In the ongoing conversations about digitization, habitual patterns of conversation and control shifted.

How innovation arises

So far I have been arguing that "organizations" are patterns of interaction between participants in complex responsive processes that tend to become routines and habits, which are continually reproduced. In this apparently closed self-referential process, patterns of talking take the form of words already spoken, embedding meaning already stabilized, where the rhetoric becomes increasingly efficient and no need is felt for a different language. In other words, already emerged identity is reproduced in our processes of interaction in the living present, becoming reinforced by "success", thus leading to the dominance of the formal, legitimate language. The language may be crystallized with very little potential for transformation. However, I have also argued that since the routines and habits are perpetually reproduced processes, there is also the possibility of variations in their reproduction. I think we begin to see how such self-referential closure generates openness when we realize that the apparent coherence of those repetitive patterns, taken to be "organizational knowledge", does not imply that those patterns are "finished or complete". This is because of the possibility of variations in reproduction and the potential for these to be amplified in the nonlinear iterative process of reproduction. At any given moment, habits and routines are temporary stabilizations in an ongoing reproduction in which there is the possibility of reformulation.

Griffin (1998) argues that the identity of an "organization" encompasses both practice and the ethical dimensions of the practice, that is, the criteria participants in a practice use to judge the quality of their actions. It is this ethical dimension that ultimately holds practitioners together and supplies the sense of belonging or identity. However, this ethical dimension is continually being transformed by participants in their practice, as they practise, in the course of their ordinary, everyday conversations in which they account to each other for their actions (Shotter, 1993). Griffin also points out that the cultural identity of an organization, the coherent "whole" of knowledge with its pragmatic and ethical aspects, is formed by the participants in their interaction while at the same time it forms them. Griffin refers to this as the paradox of culture: forming while at the same time being formed through participation. The formation of cultural identity is a self-organizing process and thus cultural identity is an emergent product of the actions and reflections of those participating in a practice. Thus "stability" is an emergent product of our responses to each other's gestures as we go on trying to make sense of being together in the living present. This "stability" and repetition become words already spoken in our daily interactions, configuring stable conversational themes. Paradoxically, innovation also emerges in such self-organizing interactions, taking the form of new words in their speaking. The problem now becomes one of how words in their speaking produce the new meaning that is innovation.

I propose to approach the problem of how new meaning is produced in conversation from the perspective of the theory of dissipative structures (Nicolis and Prigogine, 1989; Prigogine, 1996; Prigogine and Stengers, 1984).

Dissipative structures

An example of a dissipative structure is that of convection, the basis of the transfer of heat and matter in the sun and the circulation of the atmosphere and oceans that determine weather changes. A laboratory experiment may be used to explore the complexity of the phenomenon of convection, but it should be remembered that any such experiment is an idealization of, or abstraction from, the reality one is trying to understand. The experiment to do with convection involves taking a thin layer of liquid and observing its behaviour as increasing heat is applied to its base. At thermodynamic equilibrium, the temperature of this liquid is uniform throughout. Consequently, it is in a state of rest at a macro level in the sense that there are no bulk movements in it. However, at the micro level, the positions and movements of the molecules are random and hence independent of each other. They fluctuate without correlations, patterns or connections and there is therefore symmetry, in the sense that no point in the liquid differs from any other point. However, as heat is applied to the base of the liquid it sets up fluctuations that are amplified through the liquid. In other words, molecules at the base stop moving randomly and begin to move upward, so displacing those at the top, which then move down to the base of the liquid. The molecules display bulk movement in the form of a convection roll. Consequently, the symmetry of the liquid is broken in that one position in it is different from some others. At some points in the liquid, molecules are moving up and at other points they are moving down. In that sense correlations between them appear. There is now diversity at the micro level and motion at the macro level.

When a critical temperature point is reached, a new structure emerges in the liquid. Molecules move in a regular direction setting up hexagonal cells, some turning clockwise and others turning anticlockwise. The result is long-range coherence where molecular movements are correlated with each other. In the laboratory experiment, the experimenter, as external objective observer, turns up the level of the heat to the critical point but cannot impose the subsequent pattern from outside the liquid. Rather, the pattern, in which some convection rolls move in one direction and others move in the opposite direction, is produced by the internal dynamic. The direction of each roll's movement is unpredictable and cannot be determined by the experimenter. The direction taken by any one roll depends upon small chance differences in the conditions that existed as the roll formed. This unpredictability is not due simply to practical difficulties. It is intrinsic. Although a change is imposed from outside this experimental system, its response is determined by its own internal dynamic. In effect, some rolls spontaneously "choose" one direction and others spontaneously "choose" another. Prigogine calls the point at which this happens a bifurcation, and the process of spontaneous "choice" is what he means by self-organization. He calls the emergent pattern a dissipative structure.

As further heat is applied to the liquid, the symmetry of the cellular pattern is broken and other patterns emerge. Eventually the liquid reaches a turbulent state of evaporation. There is movement from one state, characterized by perfect order at the macro level and perfect symmetry at the micro level, to other states of more complex order and this occurs through a destabilizing process at bifurcation points. The system is pushed away from stable equilibrium in the form of a point attractor, through bifurcations to other attractors, such as the periodic attractor of convection rolls, and on to deterministic chaos. There is unpredictability at each bifurcation point in the sense that no subsequent state is simply deducible from the previous one. The bifurcation is a dynamic of disorder that breaks up existing pattern and it is in this dynamic of disorder the new pattern emerges.

This experiment illustrates the dynamic pattern of change that is central to the theory of dissipative structures:

- A liquid, or a gas, is held *far from equilibrium* by some *environmental constraint*, such as heat.
- In this condition, small *fluctuations*, that is, variations in molecular movements in the liquid, or gas, are *amplified* to break the microscopic *symmetry* of the entities comprising it.
- At a critical level of environmental constraint, the system reaches a *bifurcation* point. This is a point at which the system becomes unstable and has the possibility of developing along a number of different pathways.
- At this bifurcation the whole ensemble of entities *spontaneously self organizes*, in effect "choosing" a pathway, one of which could produce a new pattern, such as a laser beam. In other words, long-range *correlations* form between the entities and a new coherent pattern suddenly *emerges* without any blueprint, one that cannot be explained by, or reduced to, or predicted from, the nature of the system's component entities.
- That pattern is a *dissipative structure*, that is, one that dissipates energy or information imported from the environment so continuously renewing itself. The structure is an evolving interactive process that temporarily manifests in globally stable, irregular patterns. The pattern is continually reproduced as the heat is dissipated. This kind of pattern is essentially a paradox: symmetry and uniformity of pattern are being lost but there is still a structure; disorder is essential to the creation of the new pattern.

When it comes to the phenomenon in nature, rather than in the laboratory, there is an important difference. In the case of convection in nature there is no experimenter standing outside the system objectively observing it and turning up the heat parameter as there is in the laboratory experiment. Instead, the patterns of convection in the earth's atmosphere and oceans are caused by variations in the earth's temperature, which are in turn partially caused by the convection patterns. Outside of the laboratory, the system itself is changing the parameters and it is this that the experiment is trying to model.

This particular example is one of a dissipative structure emerging through the amplification of microscopic fluctuations in molecular movement. It is these microscopic fluctuations that impart the capacity to move from one given pattern of behaviour to another. However, the entities or molecules are all the same. When the entities are different, or diverse, as they are in human interaction, then it is possible to demonstrate that completely new patterns of behaviour, that is, novel dissipative structures, may emerge.

dissipation as a source of complex order.

What is important here, for my purposes, is that the emergence of a dissipative structure is not deducible from previous conditions. When the system is far from equilibrium, it faces multiple possibilities; the entities comprising the system engage in a collective process that none of them controls and it is the collective interaction that "discovers" new orderly behaviour. Far from equilibrium, one pattern of behaviour succeeds another and each is unpredictable. In classical thermodynamics dissipation was always associated with waste and increasing disorder. Prigogine has shown that for all open systems, and this includes all living systems, dissipation is the source of complex order. Unlike equilibrium structures, which internally damp variations and so cannot easily change, dissipative structures are precarious in that they amplify variations at bifurcation points and so can more easily change.

Dissipative structure theory offers a powerful insight into the functioning of nature: new order emerges in disorder. This is not at all consistent with the kind of view that economic theory imported from the natural sciences. Thought of from the perspective of natural law, nature works in an efficient manner in the sense that any disorder or variation is rapidly damped away. This was the basis of economic theory in which fluctuations, randomness or chaos are thought of as highly destructive and inefficient. For an economist, they are "redundant" and the efficient functioning of an economy simply removes them. Certainly, no creative importance is attached to them. The theory of dissipative structure is suggesting that such "redundancy" has a positive value for without it a system cannot produce anything creative. In his work on agent-based modelling, Kauffman (1995) also argues for the importance of redundancy in the self-organizing emergence of pattern in nature. He defines redundancy as repetitive behaviours or as the same agent actions that can be triggered by many different events. For him, redundancy means duplication, again a notion that is antithetical to economic notions of efficiency, which provides the taken-for-granted basis of mainstream thinking about innovation in human organizations. What if the notion of dissipative structures and redundancy, rather than the efficiency-based views of economic theory, were thought to form the basis of a theory of innovation? Do these notions have anything to do with humans?

Prigogine (1998) places human realities as the perfect example of systems that are far from equilibrium and possess the properties of complex systems, since the problem with human systems is typically the problem of time (life and evolution) and not of space (motion). As Nicolis argues (1989: 344):

A dynamical model of a human society begins with the realization that, in addition to its internal structure, the system is firmly embedded in an environment with which it exchanges matter, energy and information. . . . the evolution of such a system is an interplay between the behaviour of its actors and the constraints imposed by the environment. It is here that the human system finds its unique specificity. Contrary to the molecules, the "actors" of a physical–chemical system, or even ants or the members of any other animal society, human beings develop individual projects and desires. Some of these stem from anticipations about how the future might reasonably look and from guesses concerning the desires of the other actors. The difference between desired and actual behaviour acts therefore as a constraint of a new type, which, together with the environment, shapes the dynamics.

However, what could dissipation mean in human settings, and particularly in commercial organizations? Moreover, what would be the dissipative "structure" emerging out of such dissipative processes? Then, how would the processes be understood in terms of micro interactions, that is, in terms of participation in the interactions between people instead of participation in some system?

Dissipative processes in human interaction

The word "dissipative" means dispersing, dispelling, breaking up, bringing to nothing, wasting or frittering away. It is synonymous with scattering, spreading, propagating, clearing away, spending and losing. The word "structure", on the other hand, means a supporting framework, or an organized whole consisting of essential parts. It refers to the manner in which something is constructed. So, in putting these two words together, Prigogine is pointing to a form or pattern that is constructed through processes of propagation that are essentially dispersing, wasting or breaking up the very pattern they are constructing. Furthermore, he shows that such patterns emerge as completely different patterns through a process of amplifying difference, so breaking down symmetry or order as an essential prerequisite for the emergence of the new. This is a process in which pattern emerges as continuity and transformation at the same time – the pattern is forming (transforming) and being formed (transformed) in interactive processes that are essentially ones of dispersing, breaking up and wasting. The word "redundant" has similar connotations. It means superfluous and wasteful, that is, unnecessary duplication that is not required. However, what appears to be redundant may actually impart stability and robustness to a form. It is because the human brain duplicates many functions that it is robust in the sense that damage to one part can be compensated for by other parts. This is the same as the idea of loose coupling. Loosely coupled systems can continue to function when parts are damaged because no one part is absolutely essential, while tightly coupled systems cease to function when one part is damaged. I want to link the word "redundant" to the notion of diversity and fluctuations, which Prigogine shows to be essential to the emergence of new dissipative structures. What he is saying is that disorder, randomness and chaos, all normally thought to be wasteful or redundant are essential to the emergence of the new because new order emerges in the destruction of amplified diversity. One might say, therefore, that dissipative structures are characterized by "redundant diversity".

This notion of redundant diversity provides an analogy for human experience. In human communicative interaction, I suggest, redundant diversity is experienced as misunderstanding. So, the analogy with human interaction could be understood as follows. A dissipative structure in nature is really a process of construction, of continuously reproducing a particular pattern, through dissipating, that is propagating and dispersing energy or disorder (entropy). In other words, the process of construction is the dissipation of redundant diversity. By analogy, human interaction is continually reproducing patterns of understanding, that is, patterns of meaning. Patterns of meaning are being continually constructed in human interaction through a process of dissipating, that is, propagating and dispersing misunderstanding. I would define misunderstanding as the human experience of redundant diversity. In other words, human communicative interaction can be understood as a dissipative process in which what is being dissipated is redundant diversity understood as misunderstanding. At bifurcation points in human communicative interaction, redundant diversity experienced as misunderstanding arises as "fluctuations" in meanings that are amplified, as the symmetry of accepted meaning is broken up. It is in this process that the possibility for the emergence of new meaning arises. Human communicative interaction is fuelled by and serves to dissipate redundant diversity experienced as misunderstanding.

This notion of innovation as the emergence of new dissipative structures of meaning, where that emergence absolutely requires redundant diversity experienced as misunderstanding, is the complete opposite of mainstream thinking. In the rational planning strand of mainstream thinking, the innovation process is based on the removal of misunderstanding in advance. It is accorded no creative function. In the entrepreneurial/cultural systems perspective, misunderstanding is also accorded no place in the visions-and-values-driven social structure within which innovation is said to occur. Once again, misunderstanding is not accorded any constitutive, constructive role. From the complex responsive process perspective I am taking, misunderstanding fuels and is fuelled by the search for meaning and this implies that mainstream thinking is actually a way to stop innovation rather than produce it.

The dissipative process of meaning in practice

Consider now the experiences recounted in the previous two chapters from this perspective. The meaning of the galleries emerged in misunderstanding. The digitized survey emerged amidst waves of misunderstanding, that is through a process that shifted every time someone thought it was "complete and ready" and introduced it among some other "community", only to find new potential for misunderstanding that further forced the "development" of the innovation. During those processes at some points the galleries and the digitized survey "faced" bifurcation points. Both could have "gone" in some other direction. For instance, if the galleries had been a commercial success then perhaps some of the later developments would not have come to light. If the digitized survey had been "accepted" at an earlier stage as some "finished" tool it is arguable that it might not have become a control tool. However, throughout the path followed in both cases, people kept introducing them as words in new streams of conversations, punctuated by different patterns of talk, thus leading to new potentials for misunderstanding. To draw an analogy with Prigogine's theory, the constant supply of heat (redundant diversity) was present during long periods of time, thus sustaining the tendency for collapsing the innovations into a steady flow of conversation in which the meaning could stabilize and be accommodated. Instead, in both cases, but particularly in that of the digitized survey, the potential for misunderstanding was fostered as the concept and its material dimensions (the hardware and programming) were introduced into different departments and locations in the company. As people were trying to understand what it was about they kept bringing their doubts, critiques, suggestions, sometimes unrealistic expectations and wishes, instead of

innovation in redundant diversity

simply trying to adopt an economical behaviour of "getting efficient by using what it already was", thus allowing for new meaning to keep emerging out of the interaction with those who, eventually, thought it was "done". No one was really in control during these processes. Oliveira and some people in the water utility might have wished, in fact they did, that others could simply accept what "they had" to give "them", but their attempts to terminate the conversations were simply ignored and they were "sucked" back in the stream of conversations.

I suggest that dissipation, in human settings such as "organizations", occurs in participating in ordinary, everyday conversations. For example, when we contact customers, the practical reason, the economic reason, might be to inform them of the current state of their accounts or to give them information about product specifications. However, this is usually not all we do. In addition we engage in talk characterized by redundancy from the point of view of economic value or business purpose. Through these redundant communications, we acquire information about contextual variables, such as customer idiosyncrasies or customer intentions. We get information about competitors or about possible technological developments. This information, however, is not purposefully sought. At the time, we do not know what to do with it. We did not intend to get it. We did not have any instrumental goal in mind while we were engaged in such ordinary conversations. It is not "knowledge being shared" since we do not use "it" to engage in some interaction.

Most of the time, in ordinary conversations, we face some ambiguity and we sometimes have to probe for the meaning of the words pronounced by others. This happens because we engage in conversations using the pattern of talk that is pertinent to our own local interactions and life experiences, while others use different patterns of talk that have been developed in their own local interactions, as we together pattern our experiences of being together in the living present. It is because each uses a pattern of talk referring to their own life experience that the potential for misunderstanding occurs. I suggest that what is being dissipated in conversation is this misunderstanding, as people use their patterns of talk to negotiate the meaning of ambiguous, uncertain and ill-defined current or prospective events. Different patterns of talk interact to produce misunderstanding, that further interaction seeks to amplify as the misunderstanding is dissipated and the temporary stabilization of new meaning, the dissipative "structure" of meaning, emerges. I want to argue that when the level and quality (potential for misunderstanding) of redundant diversity in a conversation reaches a critical point, usually because different patterns of talk are interacting with each other, the potential arises for new patterns of meaning to emerge.

I am suggesting that when conversations are characterized by some critical state of redundant diversity in which there is a critical potential for misunderstanding, words in their speaking have the potential for transformation into new patterns of meaning. Since the conversations I am talking about are characterized by uncertainty and misunderstanding they raise anxiety in those participating. Thus, if the conversation is to continue, there must be something that allows people to overcome this anxiety and avoid the collapse of the creative potential of misunderstanding into the regular pattern of talk in words already spoken. This, I suggest is curiosity and, most important, trust. Trusting those that engage in conversations that might reach a critical level of redundant diversity and its associated potential for misunderstanding enables people to live with the anxiety arising in the frustrated expectations of finding rapid solutions and immediate support.

As part of their tasks in organizations people are expected to perform some clearly defined sequence of actions during which their behaviour is bound by rules, culture or shared expectations. This is necessary for the efficient performance of daily tasks. This is the behaviour that is validated by the legitimate pattern of interactions in companies. It is derived from the "economic purpose" of each "organization". However, while people are performing these actions, they also engage in redundantly diverse behaviour. This might arise in attempts to accommodate ambiguity, uncertainty and ill-defined outcomes of economic actions or in some current or prospective events that relate directly to the job in hand. Furthermore, people also engage in talk with their colleagues, friends, customers and other persons, about issues that do not relate to the organization or its goals and procedures.

Stacey (2000, 2001) suggests that the themes organizing the experience of being together in organizations have shadow aspects intertwined with legitimate aspects. In other words, conversations are patterned as both shadow and legitimate themes at the same time. Shadow themes can be described as patterns of talking that involve fantasizing, playing or containing anxiety and releasing frustration. Telling jokes about corporate leaders, disseminating gossip and rumours, engaging in boycotts and passive resistance are all shadow communicational interactions. However, this activity might actually be "economically productive" and lead to better solutions or to the creation of new problems, if people question what they normally do and debate alternatives to their routines.

Stacey further develops this concept as he suggests that there are many themes going on within the same complex responsive process as people continue trying to make sense of their experiences of the living present. He refers to how the experience of communicative interaction in the living present forms and is formed by many opposing themes, such as legitimate and shadow, formal and informal, conscious and unconscious, constantly in tension with each other. The official patterns of talk protected by legitimate and formal streams of conversations seek to remove redundancy in action and in talk because it is inefficient in terms of day-to-day activities. At the same time, shadow streams of communication, both conscious and unconscious, enable the potential for engaging in redundant conversations with their possibility for generating misunderstanding, the pre-condition for the emergence of new patterns of meaning.

As Watzlawick *et al.* (1967) pointed out, one cannot not communicate. Therefore, these processes are universal. As people engage in more circular and stable interrelations with other people aimed at reducing redundancy and doing more of the same, they will inevitably engage in dissipation (non-economical conversations) through which innovation might emerge. Thus, innovation becomes a property of communicational interactions of everyday life. This is the main argument of this book and the point of departure from mainstream ways of interpreting innovation in organizations that were described in Chapter 2.

Innovation is not a function or a rational choice but a potential in all communicative interaction. Thus, our experience of being together does not comprise the "need" to adapt to some environment. Rather, we might innovate and through these innovations, we might find new enhanced balances between our joint actions and some "outside" conditions. New principles of adaptation are not out there to be uncovered. Through new streams of conversations, people might build the perception that change is required or imperative. They may try to reduce changes to a minimum in order to protect their identity and their stability, and they may try new things. If these things work, they will incorporate this novel behaviour as part of their own identity, thus reaching a new stabilization, passing through a kind of phase transition to reach a new degree of order that will inevitably be subverted by yet other conversations.

What innovation is

If innovation emerges from conversations characterized by critical levels of redundant diversity, how do we account for the existence of the intentional, purposeful activities that go on in, for example, R&D departments? How do we account for structured projects, for new product development and for the networks of companies that intentionally establish alliances to share development costs or to develop a new technology?

visible phase of innovation

I argue that such activities are the visible phases of innovation that are preceded by a long period of conversations and ambiguous actions. The structured activities take place only when new words have already become part of the official pattern of talk. It is new knowledge already stabilized. It enables organized and purposeful action, which is already measurable against some yardstick. It is acting for which one can set milestones.

invisible phase of innovation

Prior to this phase, I argue that there must be communicative interaction involving speculation, imagination and fantasy. This process occurs among different people and in different locations. Since no purpose is detectable at the beginning of a particular conversational sequence from which an innovation emerges, because such purpose itself emerges in conversation, anyone within an organization might engage in this kind of talk. Speculation, imagination and fantasy might arise anywhere: from conferences people have attended, from magazines, from analogies drawn from other social settings, from social practices. As conversations progress some of the themes might recur. They become a pattern in such conversations. If this happens there then follows a period of intense negotiation of meaning. The outcome of these negotiations is that alternative explanations are increasingly ruled out. As new words become agreed upon, eventually some of the original contributors might withdraw as they disagree with what is stabilizing.

phase H/w Inv & V

The acceptance of the newly stabilized meaning might spread among groups or communities of practice. They acquire a new instrumental dimension. They are no longer just words, but instead they are part of a new pattern of conversation. They might be acted upon, in the sense that they might alter some material reality. If these new actions are supported by those who have the power to authorize the use of resources, openly or covertly, then experiments start. The results of these experiments will form the input to new redundant conversations. As new solutions emerge, there will be further questioning of novel experiments compared to the merits of old solutions that have become routine. If the outcome of experiments becomes a socially accepted "fact" then it will be incorporated in the legitimate pattern of talk in the current activities organizations engage in with the expectation of improving their viability. It is then that these activities become located in precise geographic settings, such as R&D. The process is, thus, self-organizing since no one can control the course of conversations, no matter how powerful they are, although they might be able to terminate them. No one can control or shape the output since it is emergent. There is no individual hero at this stage.

However, this process, as it enters a more stable and ordered pattern of interaction, tends to be reified and this "hides" the very nature of the process itself. Innovation is, in my view, the new meaning that is the emergent product of the dissipation occurring in conversations characterized by redundant diversity experienced as misunderstanding. The new meaning may be embodied in some new "thing" that is apparently detached from the messy process of its creation.

Furthermore, people tend to become detached from the emergent process of new meaning by their tendency to reconstruct past processes as coherent, logical and individually centred.

Conclusion

I have been arguing that at any one time an "organization" is patterns of words already spoken, routines and procedures already formulated, all of which together constitute a coherent enough "whole" to enable, while also constraining, day-to-day action. However, this "whole" is not complete or finished because an "organization" is required to respond to gestures made by other "organizations" and participants in complex responsive processes. The "whole" is also not complete because of the ethical dimension of human action requiring them constantly to negotiate and justify their actions to each other. Furthermore, any stability in those patterns will be temporary because this "whole", or culture, is both formed by and forms the individuals participating in it at the same time. This "whole" is both stability and instability at the same time.

I have also argued that a helpful way to think about the process through which knowledge changes in an organization is to take the dissipative structure perspective. I suggest that conversation is the pattern that constructs social realities and that, therefore, we need to say something about the dynamics of conversations. Conversational dynamics are stable when they take place in words already spoken, that is, patterns of talk with meaning patterns already established and stabilized. Such patterns of talk are characterized by low levels of redundant diversity in the sense that the conversation is instrumental, leading rapidly to action having an economic value to the agents concerned. There is very little potential for misunderstanding. Such patterns of talk may evolve incrementally, but do not lead to significant change, that is, innovation.

I have then argued that when the level of redundant diversity increases, that is, when people engage in conversations not driven by the demands of immediate action having economic value and when they interact with each other from different patterns of talk, the potential for misunderstanding amplifies. When this reaches a critical level, the intensive search for understanding leads to the emergence of new meaning. A new pattern of talk, embedding a new pattern of meaning, emerges and can only be sustained while the misunderstanding is dissipating. The dissipative structure is meaning, that is, the new pattern of talk, that which is being dissipated, that which is holding the conversation far from equilibrium, is the misunderstanding. Since this misunderstanding provokes anxiety, the far-from-equilibrium conversational dynamic can only be sustained when those engaging in it trust each other enough. I suggest that this is a radically different way of understanding the process of innovation since it puts misunderstanding at the heart of the possibility of innovation. Innovation is almost always equated with understanding, thereby downplaying, or even ignoring, the vital importance of misunderstanding.

The next chapter presents the story of another innovation to illustrate the theoretical perspective described in this chapter.

6 Innovation and the reconfiguration of power relations

* The story of an electronic product catalogue
* The transformation of meaning
* The take off of the product catalogue
* Conclusion

In the last chapter, I outlined a way of thinking about organizations as complex responsive processes of relating between people. It is in these processes of communicative interaction and power relating that organizational and individual identities emerge as continuity and potential transformation. It is this potential for transformation that is the origin of innovation. The process of innovation is the continual nonlinear iterative reproduction of themes patterning the experience of being and doing together. That process is one of simultaneously iterating continuity and the potential for transformation. The iteration simultaneously damps and amplifies difference, that is, variations around habitual themes organizing the experience of being and doing together. To put it another way, the process is one of dissipating redundant diversity experienced as misunderstanding. Meaning, the basis of being and doing together, can be understood as analogous to dissipative structures. As such, patterns of meaning are sustained by the process of dissipating redundant diversity experienced as misunderstanding in communicative interaction. In the last chapter, I illustrated this theoretical perspective with examples from the stories of innovation presented in Chapters 3 and 4. In this chapter, I want to extend that illustration by means of another narrative about innovation.

The story of an electronic product catalogue

I came to be involved with the innovation described in this chapter when a friend invited me to dinner at her former husband's home. She said that he was interested in chaos theory and felt that we would enjoy talking together. I accepted the invitation and went to Carlos Campos' home, where we enjoyed a pleasant dinner. Carlos mentioned that his organization was developing a "revolutionary" product, namely, an electronic product catalogue, which I might be interested in. After some fine cigars and brandy, in addition to an extremely interesting account of Carlos' life in the navy and of the way in which he had started his business, I knew I had to find out more about the innovation he had mentioned. I was then introduced to Guillermo Barrera, a key figure in the development of the electronic catalogue, who also proved to be a most interesting character.

I first made contact with people in Carlos' and Guillermo's company (CEP) in March 1996 and continued talking to them until May 1998. During that time, I read many company documents such as memos, commercial leaflets, reports presented to meetings with partners, and catalogue reference manuals. I took part in formal meetings, where I talked to the leaders of companies collaborating with CEP and with the executives of a large retailer working on the introduction of the catalogue. I also attended many formal and informal presentations on the new catalogue. However, most of my time was spent in conversations with people working in CEP while they were going about their daily tasks. I was able to witness daily routines: phone calls, decisions being taken, debates among company members, debugging of programs, corrections to the system, speculations, attributions, emotions, and so on. The technical language created a major difficulty for me and I tried to deal with this by reading some textbooks and talking to some independent IT consultants. What was most helpful, however, was working with and talking to the people in CEP. I soon realized that the technical language also caused problems for them and that we all dealt with our lack of understanding in much the same way.

The background

Over the past twenty years the pattern of consumer goods distribution has changed dramatically in Portugal. Although they still account for 100,000 jobs, convenient local stores have been increasingly displaced by shopping malls and hypermarkets. Portuguese, French and Dutch companies, attracted by soaring sales available to first entrants, have constructed large stores with parking spaces for thousands of cars, so invading every small village in the country, making it nearly impossible for small local businesses to survive. Apart from creating employment problems, this development has other cultural and social implications. The disappearance of local stores removes important venues where local people meet and talk to each other, so developing a sense of local identity. Senior and poorer citizens lose the most because they find it difficult to travel to the big commercial areas and so feelings of isolation grow. Not surprisingly, therefore, what may seem to be simply an economic trend has now become an important political matter.

The huge retail shops have significant logistics problems. There are typically around 50,000 product references and bar-coded labels in such stores, and severe price competition between the stores means that prices are always changing, requiring amendments to the product references. Other specific parameters such as suppliers' lead times, minimum order quantities, different VAT regimes according to country of origin of the product and brand names, all add complexity to the process of information management.

The idea

In late 1989, Guillermo, an Argentinean, was working for Digital in Brazil, when Sonae, one of the largest industrial groups in Portugal, hired him to take care of their information systems, which connected to more than twenty manufacturing facilities and offices in different countries. His task was to establish a compatible communication and information system that allowed documents to be exchanged without the loss of the original document form or any information. Guillermo's first step was to contact suppliers of information and communication services in Portugal. In talking to them, he made a number of important personal acquaintances and built up a good knowledge of companies, products and technologies in the country. By 1992, Sonae's industrial division was in decline and so Guillermo was moved to the distribution division to take responsibility for the information systems of several hypermarkets that Sonae owned and managed.

The department Guillermo found himself in charge of had established an internal communication platform prior to his arrival. This involved passing every purchase order from individual stores to a centralized purchasing department, which then passed the orders on to suppliers. However, this was a time and labour consuming activity of price verification, packaging specification, and promotional campaign negotiation and ordering by phone, fax or mail. Guillermo had experience with the UN's Electronic Data Interchange (EDI) standards, acquired in his Digital days, and thought it would be possible to apply EDI standards to form direct connections between the shops and the suppliers, thereby making ordering more efficient. However, retailers and suppliers did not classify products in the same way on their databases. A supplier brand might cover a number of packaging options, with different physical dimensions and corresponding bar codes, but retailer's information databases were often not updated to reflect all this information. Technically, this meant that their databases were not aligned, and this stood in the way of Guillermo's desire to establish direct connections between them.

In late 1993, a magazine called *Distribuição Hoje* (Distribution Today) organized a conference of suppliers and large retailers and invited Guillermo to speak at it. Guillermo knew that the magazine published a printed catalogue of products, which became obsolete as soon as it was published because of rapid changes in product specification. In his speech, Guillermo called for the establishment of an electronic catalogue of all products that could be rapidly updated and used by all companies in the distribution chain. This would, of course, enable Guillermo's department to realize his intention of making the direct links between shops and suppliers. Some of Sonae's major competitors immediately backed this idea and indicated that they would buy such a service if the magazine publisher developed it. Subsequently, Guillermo organized meetings between the publisher and General Electric, the only company with expertise in this area at the time. The purpose of the meeting was to discuss establishing a company that would design and operate an electronic product catalogue service. However these efforts came to nothing because, according to Guillermo, people in the publishing company were too "stuck to paper".

By the end of 1994, Guillermo was dissatisfied with his prospects at Sonae and he moved to Lisbon where he worked as a consultant to distribution businesses. He worked for a year as a consultant for a large retail group and at the same time he continued to lecture and give seminars on the idea of an electronic product catalogue. Wherever he went, he discussed the idea but his attempts to develop this theme in ongoing conversations met with little interest on the part of powerful people in the distribution chain. In March 1995, at one of his seminars, an engineer who owned a small company providing computer services, showed interest in his idea. He introduced Guillermo to Carlos Campos. The three met to discuss how they might establish a company to create the catalogue. Guillermo had developed his thoughts and presented them to the other two. His ideas on what a product catalogue should be and how it should be developed were as follows.

The lead company that Guillermo and his partners would set up would issue catalogue licenses and charge the suppliers for each product reference inscribed in the catalogue. However, the knowledge required to build such an ambitious information system would have to come from many diverse areas of expertise. Since no single company possessed the required range of competencies, it would be necessary to establish an alliance of leading companies in the areas of expertise required. The partners would not directly profit from catalogue revenues, but from selling a variety of services to catalogue users such as hardware, database software, software for linking the catalogue with integrated information management systems, communication links and tools, mailboxes and digital telephones lines.

Guillermo proposed inviting two competitors from each field of expertise to join the alliance. There were, in his mind, three good reasons for this strategic alliance policy. First, it would prevent the catalogue from becoming bogged down in problems between customers and any one of the alliance companies. The fact that there would be a number of companies in the alliance would present future customers with options and a degree of freedom that would preserve the catalogue. Guillermo was very sensitive to this issue because he had been in the position of both information technology supplier and customer. The second benefit of the alliance policy would be two different sources of know-how for each class of technical problem. The development of the catalogue would thus not be impeded if one partner were to pull out. The third benefit was that if they could participate in the venture, no one company would be tempted to develop the catalogue on their own.

Another main guideline was that the catalogue should be based, as much as possible, on standard protocols. Acceptance of protocols that people were already working with would decrease resistance to change and so speed up the introduction phase of the product. Yet another main guideline was that the catalogue should target the European market.

There was an emerging trend for locally based retailers to buy internationally, reinforced by major multinational manufacturers moving out of Portugal to concentrate their industrial facilities in France and Spain. Furthermore, local retailers tended to buy a large variety of product specialties, mainly food products, from small manufacturers all over Europe. This European dimension led to the commitment to build a multilingual and multi-currency version of the catalogue.

However, this strategy did not please the engineer, who viewed the venture as an opportunity for his small company to grow. He wanted the exclusive right to install all the PCs that customers would require to connect to the catalogue database. Guillermo and Carlos did not expect the small company to be able to respond to the quantity of work that the catalogue might trigger and since the engineer insisted on his demand, they excluded him from the project. Later, he was to approach a company called Nielsen and bring them into contact with *Distribuição Hoje* to develop a similar information system.

"Catalogo Electrónico de Produtos Base de Dados, S.A." (CEP) was finally established in July 1995, with Guillermo holding 32 per cent of the shares, Carlos and two other partners from Pararede holding 17 per cent each and a further 17 per cent reserved for EAN, an independent association that governs bar coding and standards in Europe. It was thought that the last named organization would add visibility and credibility to the catalogue. At first, CEP operated from Guillermo's attic and the staff consisted of two of his former students at the University of Minho where he had taught artificial intelligence. In January 1996, CEP moved to offices on the second floor of the Pararede building and, by July, Guillermo had organized a formal meeting of major companies, some of which eventually became partners in the venture. These "knowledge investors" consisted of: IBM; Microsoft; Oracle; Gupta Technologies; SSA; Telepac; Portugal Telecom; Synon Inc; Informix; Eurociber; Amdahl; and Pararede.

The purpose of the catalogue was to enable the on-line display of all the products that hundreds of suppliers had to offer. The idea was that the registration of a product on the catalogue would cover the brand name and bar code, information on units of sale, size and dimensions, models, ordering quantities, packaging formats and options, warranties, after-sale support, warnings, special conditions of use, conditions of storage and shelf life, and even an audio-image of the product. This information was to be loaded by suppliers. However, prior to being accepted in the catalogue, the information would be checked automatically by a routine program in artificial intelligence that tests the registration for possible inconsistencies or incongruent data, such as bar-code duplication or other mistakes, for example. The catalogue was to be a platform that allowed, indeed depended upon, suppliers placing information about their products, saving the time, labour and cost of sending it by fax or any other direct communication for hundreds of customers. In addition, the system would enable a direct connection between supplier and retailer through private and secure mailboxes.

Retailers would then be able to select products from the catalogue and pass them on to their ordering systems, placing the orders directly with the supplier through the catalogue communication links. This operation would require a buyer to fill in a form that was compatible with the forwarding services of the supplier. It would be technically possible to invoice and pay through this system, linked through SIBS, a company that manages all electronic transactions for the banks through the ATM network. Ultimately, the catalogue would be a data-warehouse that might be used to monitor, in real time, the sales that were being made at any point-of-sale in any store. The system would allow the processing of information from automatic scanning of bar-coded products and this would enable suppliers to have real-time access to information about sales and inventories of hundreds of retailers. This might lead to supplier management of the retailer's inventory on a "just-in-time" basis. It could also serve to monitor the progression of new products.

The catalogue was truly an innovative concept as it anticipated what we presently know as e-markets, e-commerce and Customer Relationship Management.

The development of the catalogue

At an early stage, a formal procedure was agreed to develop the catalogue in five phases:

1 A static text catalogue. The task here was developing the database, browsing programs, and communication links.
2 Data collection of sales. The task here was building a data-warehouse and an on-line connection with bar-code scanning processes in retailers' cashiers.
3 Building an information-sharing platform. This would enable vendor inventory management.

4 Adding images and sounds (multimedia) to the catalogue.
5 Electronic ordering, invoicing and paying. The task here was to establish safe conditions for operating through the catalogue.

From the beginning, the idea was a very ambitious one and presumed that the catalogue would be the platform connecting all the different information and management systems that are operated in the distribution chain. It aimed to become the central information forwarding system, connecting peripheral systems such as the programs used in the stores to optimize space on the shelves. Based on the idea that the catalogue must be an independent product, Guillermo selected as many information standards as possible, so that the catalogue could be approved and recommended by all the institutions that regulate the "supply chain". These procedures were supposed to render the catalogue independent of databases, of operating systems, and of communications protocols.

Because he had been experimenting for quite some time, Guillermo had already completed the product conception phase with a feasibility study on the possibilities of using EDI and of integrating other technologies with it. This was done in Guillermo's attic with two of his former students, until they were able to move to the offices of Pararede – a move they made because they assumed that it would not be credible to talk about a company that was setting out to revolutionize the procedures of an entire industry from someone's attic. However, the space provided by Pararede had to be renovated and adapted, so for quite some time, CEP developed the catalogue in the midst of construction work, often overcharging the power circuits and causing daily system shut downs. There was an unbearable level of noise and dust, plus the loss of programming because of power shut downs. This environment was far from being adequate for R&D efforts.

Just before the move in December of 1995, the "knowledge partners" were sent a detailed specification of the work that they would be required to perform. This plan of work set out standard steps, such as: definition of product concept; global design, implementation of development following clear cycles of design-prototype-testing of components; and integration tests, loading tests, and system pilot trials. Even though this formal plan was supplied to the partners and was used to schedule the work, it was expected that unforeseen problems would occur. Nevertheless, this logical sequence of activities was enough to generate an over-optimistic expectation about the dates of completion and commercial launching of the catalogue.

After the first tests, it was realized that a product information sheet could contain more than 30,000 characters, which proved to be too long to be easily carried by the selected EDI protocol. This was an unpredictable nuisance and delayed the project for at least for three months. There were two options to consider: either the catalogue product sheet could be reduced; or, the standard could be changed to accommodate the needs of the Portuguese catalogue. The decision was to explore changing the standards. Since then, more than ten requests for improving the standards have been made and accepted. This unusual number of change requests led staff at EAN Europe to wonder what was happening in Portugal.

SIBS (the company established by the banks) was selected to be the "service provider", meaning that the main database was lodged in its highly reliable and available computers. It was felt that potential users would perceive SIBS as the most reliable host for the catalogue and so be reassured that potential system shut down would not present a serious risk. In addition, the fact that such a prestigious organization was involved in the project would enhance the venture's reputation. It was the personal relationship between Guillermo and the general manager of Amdahl Portugal that proved instrumental in securing the participation of SIBS.

As the work progressed, some potential customers stressed the benefits that access to product images would bring. These conversations led to a decision to make an early start with what was supposed to be the fourth phase, since using multimedia technology was, at the time, a lesser problem than it was presumed to be at the beginning of the process. Additionally, Guillermo's membership of EDI committees allowed him to participate in the conversations regarding the future regulations for EDI image transmission. In March 1996 a pilot prototype was ready for testing.

Coincidentally, at this time, the international congress of EAN was taking place in Lisbon. Guillermo, through his informal networking activities, discovered in which hotel the meetings would take place. His company rented the next room and made presentations of the catalogue during the congress. This proved to be a good move because at least Brazilian EAN officials showed some interest. Later that year, the President of EAN Brazil and the director of a large retail group came to Portugal and decided to acquire the catalogue as soon as it was ready. However, this posed an unexpected problem, namely, the cost of telephone communications between the users in Brazil and the database in Portugal. From the start, the catalogue had been developed as a product to be positioned in Europe. That was why it was to work in a multilingual and multi-currency mode. However, the cost of telephone connection had not really been taken into account. The request from Brazil directed attention to this problem and led to consideration of using the Internet, because of its cheap telephone connections, as a prospective carrier for the catalogue. This led to concerns about the lack of security on the Internet, since communications through this network are easy targets for hackers. The technical solution chosen to solve the security problem was the adoption of the ISOCOR encryption program. This was the "natural" choice since it came from the same company that was developing the communication technology. Another surprise occurred. The ISOCOR encryption program did not prove to be fully secure for the communication of EDI messages. Much work was lost and this time, instead of proposing adaptations or improvements in the standards, the effort was abandoned when SIBS suggested the use of another tool, which they had developed for credit cards and for smart cards.

In late 1996, CEP increased its capital and in February 1997, the catalogue entered a phase of final verification. Three more programmers were hired to conduct procedures of database management, of quality assurance and "full load" testing.

The transformation of meaning

I want to pause for a moment and consider how one might make sense of the story so far. As with Oliveira's story of drainage pipes in Chapter 3 and that of the digitized survey in Chapter 4, it is possible to point to many aspects of this story of an electronic catalogue that support interpretations from either or both of the mainstream perspectives on innovation discussed in Chapter 2. There is certainly much evidence of rational decision making, planning and programming. There is also considerable evidence to support an entrepreneurial/social interpretation. Guillermo could quite plausibly be described as a typical entrepreneur with an inspiring vision and charismatic leadership qualities. From early 1994 to early 1997 when the product catalogue reached the stage of product verification, there was continuous political activity taking the form of negotiations with backers to form and operate the company, with "knowledge partners" to provide expertise, with regulatory authorities with potential supplier and retailer customers, and with potential rivals.

My argument, however, is that while they are valid, these interpretations are quite limiting in making sense of how the innovation was evolving.

Understanding of the process is enhanced, I suggest, by thinking of the rational planning and the entrepreneurial/social activities as aspects of much wider processes of communicative interaction and power relating. From this perspective, the story of the electronic catalogue is understood as processes of continual reproduction of meaning as both continuity and transformation at the same time. My rather linear account of the development of the catalogue makes the story readily understandable, but it no more than hints at the ordinary day-to-day conversations in which those developing the catalogue accomplished their work. Although I had to start the story somewhere, for example, with Guillermo's arrival in Portugal, I tried to indicate that this was not really the beginning, because Guillermo's previous experience was to prove to be among the enabling conditions of the innovation. The same was true of other actors in the story, from Carlos Campos to the large retailers, their suppliers and the declining numbers of small retailers. Throughout the story, I have pointed to networks of contacts made, for example, by giving a speech at a conference or joining a standards committee. The ideas that Guillermo and others were forming were emerging in their conversations with each other and as they conversed and negotiated, patterns of power relations emerged and shifted between them, all as aspects of the process of developing the electronic catalogue.

The evolution of the catalogue involved different technologies and this led to problems in people understanding each other. For example, sometimes when the developers were discussing the capabilities of some piece of hardware their conversation would reach an impasse. One person would simply state that a given piece of equipment had some possibility, while another would claim that it was completely unsuitable, without either really justifying the position being taken. Anxiety levels would rise, some would withdraw emotionally and others would propose talking about it later. Or the most senior person present might resolve the matter, simply stating what would happen without justifying the decision in any way. Quite often, the language used in these discussions meant very little to me and it seemed to others as well. Since the pieces of programming came from different sources, sometimes nothing happened after "pushing the button". One would say, "it should be OK, it worked before", while another might reply, "well, nothing is happening, so it is not working here". Heightened emotion could then easily disrupt communication.

So, despite the efforts to base everything on the propositional knowledge of standards and procedures in an attempt to remove misunderstanding, it seemed to be occurring all the time. To deal with the constantly arising misunderstanding people resorted to informal conversations. Sometimes people got together and tried to understand what was "wrong", and when they did this they explored the problem in a trial-and-error way. When some kind of understanding began to emerge the emotional atmosphere changed – it felt good to be together and previous disagreements about the meaning of the words they had been using faded away. The progress of the work depended not on some procedure but on their personal relationships with each other. The work was emerging in their interaction with each other.

The problem of installing the catalogue in SIBS, for instance, was not a decision taken in advance that then guided the ensuing actions. It was the emergent outcome of ongoing conversations between Guillermo and his friends at the company that supplies SIBS computers. After the agreement was made, the positive points of this decision were rationalized into the advantages that are now emphasized.

The whole point of the catalogue was to enhance predictability between suppliers and retailers, bringing greater order to their messy relationship. However, the process of developing it was itself messy, in the sense that each step taken usually resulted in another messy problem that needed to be sorted out. Even chance events brought more complications. The Brazilian interest, for instance, was greeted as a very important event, yet it "forced" CEP to develop a number of solutions for problems they had not foreseen. This led to the interest in placing the catalogue on the Internet, for example. It was realized that instead of transferring updates separately in each working station of the catalogue in the customer's offices, with all the problems of different software, the updates might be done through the Internet. However, that had implications for the programming language used so that even as the project was moving towards completion, it was already clear that there would have to be another generation of the catalogue, this time using the JAVA language to enable use of the Internet.

The motivation to participate in the innovation process identified by some of the companies was the expectation that they would be able to reap some "lateral" benefits. One example of this was the hope that a better understanding of the needs of the distribution chain would enable them to sell products in addition to the catalogue. The catalogue was not only built by fusing multiple technologies, but also enabled a common learning process for the different partners as they shared their knowledge as well as their expectations. Thus, what emerged out of the process was a more robust understanding of the pattern of talk used in the distribution chain, as well as an understanding of other patterns of talk spoken in the IT industry since they were "forced" to integrate different technologies. Therefore, in order to have their software solutions "talking" to each other they were forced to engage in dialogue within different patterns of talk.

The planning of tasks was constantly defeated by the rapid pace of change in IT, as well as by unexpected and unintended events. The Internet, the demands for EDI standard improvements and the encryption problems were discovered as the process went on.

These conversations, replicated daily in the living present of many local situations, were the evolving meaning of the electronic catalogue. There was much continuity in this meaning; at the same time that meaning was transforming, for example, as the standards were renegotiated, SIBS was involved and the prospect of locating the catalogue on the Internet emerged. What the story I have told only hints at is the often duplicated, seemingly wasteful activities I witnessed people engaging in. I briefly mentioned the difficulties people from different information technology backgrounds had in understanding each other's terminology as they worked together to realize a completely new information system that required inputs from all of them. There was indeed a great deal of redundant diversity experienced as misunderstanding. It became clear to me that it was just this daily misunderstanding that drove people to engage in more intensive conversations, which served to dissipate the misunderstanding and so sustain a fragile, easily destroyed, dissipative structure of meaning.

Notice how this innovation involved interaction between people across many organizations. It makes no sense to talk about a shared culture promoting innovative behaviour. Furthermore it is clear that no one of the actors involved could choose what was to happen. Throughout, the innovation was emerging in communicative interaction patterned by ideological themes expressed in shifting patterns of power relations and the dynamics of inclusion and exclusion.

Consider now the further evolution of the electronic product catalogue.

The take off of the product catalogue

From mid 1996 on, the idea of the catalogue had been promoted to suppliers, retailers and various institutional players who might have some influence. There was also the need to motivate the "knowledge partners" when they became uneasy about increasing costs and lengthening time frames, due to unplanned events and inability to match optimistic expectations. Meetings were held to calm the partners when their expectations of a fast return were not met. The catalogue was presented as a win-win game in which no one would be "hurt". Suppliers would not have to develop "point to point" proprietary solutions with major customers and retailers would not have to develop their own catalogues. There were also national political implications. Both the government and the small traders' associations were concerned with the erosion of small business due to the growing power of the major retailers. They welcomed the catalogue and there was talk of financial support for small local businesses to use it. The catalogue came to be understood as a transparent and democratic "equalizer" of information access, yet another example of the transformation of meaning.

However, despite all the activity, the catalogue was not yet a product in the market place. Technical problems had been solved, partners were selected on the basis of being reliable and credible, political lobbying had gone much better then expected, and yet major retailers, despite declaring enthusiastic support, in which they were followed by suppliers, were not installing the catalogue. At least six months had been spent playing a game of "if they do it, then I will do it". For the catalogue to be perceived as a real solution that would be adopted, it was required that at least one of the leading retailers should clearly send a message of adoption. At this point big retailers, at least those who were supposed to be able to trigger the process of adoption and set the wheel turning, were still hesitating. Even if they were preparing for the adoption of the catalogue, aligning their databases, proceeding to install the communications platforms, the fact remained that "selling" the idea of a catalogue did not prove as easy as had been hoped.

Some of the retailers were pushing the suppliers to acquire a proprietary solution that would enable them to connect with only one retailer. The technology chosen was Lotus Notes. Even though IBM was involved in the development of the catalogue as a "knowledge partner", they were also selling and promoting this solution and their own technology. For people in CEP the attitude of suppliers was difficult to understand. The catalogue would benefit the suppliers because it would make it unnecessary to manage individual connections with their major customers and it could bring small independent retailers into the system, a move that might shift the balance of power back to the suppliers. Small retailers might be used to launch and try out new products. The reason for launching new products through the large groups resides mainly in the speed of communication processes with these customers. Moreover, the size of their customer base allows an easy assessment of the reactions to a new product. With the catalogue, informing a large number of small retailers becomes a faster process. It does not involve a process of communicating the product to every single company. In addition, if these small traders were brought into the system they could be willing to cooperate and to become a very effective net of information about consumer behaviour.

However, even though suppliers hoped that the catalogue might have the effects described above, they were still waiting for one of the "Big Five" retailers to impose the system on them. Meanwhile, the retailers said that if the suppliers started filling the catalogue they would adopt it. Overcoming this stalemate would require a great deal of patience and persuasion. The marketing strategy was revised in response to these problems. Initially, CEP had two people going around suppliers and retailers with a catalogue demonstration. Invariably people agreed that the product was excellent and that it would be a wonderful improvement on current procedures. Nevertheless, this effort did not translate into any real progress and no sale was achieved. Formal and informal agreements were then made with some "knowledge partners" so that they would become catalogue promoters and sellers. However, these partners were not effective in promoting the catalogue even though they had a direct interest in selling several associated services once the catalogue was installed. Then the retailers who had already decided to adopt the catalogue complained that CEP was not pressing the suppliers to start filling the catalogue with their product information. A general manager was hired in February 1997, and together with another person started directly contacting the suppliers.

One of the major concerns that surfaced in conversations during this phase was the problem of price differentiation. Theoretically, this is an illegal action. Laws within the EU and Portugal forbid companies from practicing non-transparent price policies. However, in practical terms, price differentiation is a cornerstone of commercial activity in the supply chain. Within an hour, a range of prices could be used to order the same product: there might be a special price for the opening of a new store, a regular order to two different stores, and a promotional campaign in another, all at different prices.

Finally, it became clear that people were worried about the access CEP would have to price information through its management of the catalogue. Even with the assurance that prices could remain outside the catalogue and be sent directly to private mailboxes, through direct communication, this issue became an unforeseen difficulty. At the start of the project, it had been argued that including prices in the standard product information would be a major benefit provided by the catalogue, because price updates account for more then 90 per cent of the changes in product data. However, this idea had to be abandoned because people were reluctant to store sensitive information in this form, even if an encryption system with passwords could be devised to accommodate direct and private connections between a retailer and a supplier. This was surely a major emergent transformation in the meaning of the electronic product catalogue.

Another issue was the suppliers' desire to have access to the names of those retailers who browsed through their pages and the desire of retailers to remain anonymous. So far, the will of retailers has prevailed. Another difficulty emerged because the engineer who introduced Guillermo and Carlos approached the Nielsen organization saying that Guillermo wanted to compete with them. Subsequently he visited retailers informing them that he and Nielsen would develop a catalogue that would compete with Guillermo's catalogue. Although this angered people at CEP, it turned out to have unexpected promotional benefits in that it increased awareness of the catalogue.

Recently the catalogue is moving forward as far as its adoption in Portugal is concerned. However, its largest success so far is the adoption of the catalogue as a tool by the powerful Spanish telephone company, Telefónica, a development that had much to do with the entrance of Pararede into the Spanish market. The catalogue is currently being promoted in nearly all EU countries and seems to have promising prospects.

The catalogue was originally defined as a common, transparent and independent platform of information. It aimed at being the minimal common denominator for supplier–retailer logistics data. Initially, it was assumed at CEP that people process information rationally and that was why they presented the catalogue as a transparent and independent platform, stressing the benefits for everyone. However, later events were to reveal the political nature of this innovation. It became clear that this innovation would have an impact on the power balance across the entire industry. From a purely rational perspective, the catalogue provided a more logical and efficient logistics procedure. However, rationality was only part of the process. More important, it turned out, were the different perceptions, expectations and fears of each of the players. They were socially constructing a reality that was not simply rational. For instance, Guillermo argues that multinational suppliers like Unilever and Procter & Gamble seemed to be caught in a "self fulfilling prophecy". They watched their power being eroded and yet did not embrace the catalogue as a tool for regaining some of that power. Use of the catalogue could shift the power balance back to the smaller stores and so weaken the hold of large retailers and suppliers, and yet they did not vigorously seek to adopt the catalogue.

Conclusion

I suggest that the story of the electronic catalogue shows how it is too simple to argue that an innovation is the realization of any one individual's intention, whether it be cast as a goal or a vision. How an innovation evolves depends upon the interaction of many people's choices. In this sense innovation emerges in self-organizing interaction between many people. The story told in this chapter also supports the view that innovations inevitably shift power relations and the ideologies that support them, raising the possibility of responses that will alter the meaning of the innovation. Innovation is not simply new things or new ways of acting but transformations in patterns of meaning. Both individual and collective identities are patterns of meaning and innovation therefore transforms identities.

7 Conclusion

- **Conversation as the process of dissipating meaning**
- **Relationship as the condition for living with anxiety**
- **The emergence of meaning**
- **The institutionalization of meaning**
- **The challenge to the institutionalization of meaning**

When one thinks of organizations as complex responsive processes, one focuses attention on the constitutive and constructive processes of human relating, of human communicative interaction figured as power relations. The conversation people continually engage in as they work becomes perhaps the most important feature of organizational life. It is in conversational processes that organizational and individual identities emerge as continuity and potential transformation. Innovation comes to be understood as the process of transforming both collective and individual identities. What fuels and is fuelled by the process of transformation is misunderstanding. To conclude this book I want to draw out some of the key features of innovation understood in this way.

Conversation as the process of dissipating meaning

One of the most important common patterns that can be identified in the three innovation stories told in this book is the following. The new meaning that came to be embedded in each innovation cannot be located at any particular point in time or space, nor can it be located simply in one individual, even when one person was a very prominent figure in the story. The ideas did not occur as a direct product of a purposeful search triggered by the perception of some problem to solve. The ideas did not result from a sequential process that was laid out in advance as part of the legitimate control systems of an organization: the process was not one of controlled movement from an old to new already specified way of doing things. The ideas did not present themselves as new meaning already stabilized as a whole. Instead, the ideas were a product of streams of conversations, characterized by high levels of redundant diversity experienced as misunderstanding that extended over long periods of time. Oliveira and Guillermo spent years engaging in conversational activities, muddling through debates as their views and desires clashed with those of other people before anything like an innovation began to emerge. In a similar vein, the digitized survey was also the fruit of extended conversations before it was actually realized, and it is even more obvious here that Epal's innovation cannot be identified with a single promoter.

I suggest that we can understand these experiences if we see new meaning (knowledge) as that which emerges from self-organizing conversations characterized by critical levels of redundant diversity/ misunderstanding. I am also suggesting that we can think of such conversations as far-from-equilibrium phenomena, in the sense that different patterns of talk continuously interact with each other so as to amplify the potential for misunderstanding. This far-from-equilibrium conversational process is one in which those participating are able to hold the anxiety that misunderstanding generates and continue trying to transform that misunderstanding into new mutually meaningful patterns of talk. I suggest that we can think of such new mutually meaningful patterns of talk as equivalent to dissipative structures, where what is being dissipated, what is sustaining the dissipative structure, is the misunderstanding generated by continuously bringing into the conversation words from different patterns of talk. What I want to stress here is the point that novelty, innovation, emerges when redundant diversity experienced as misunderstanding is at some critical level. I mean by this that no immediately coherent action is possible based on the words being spoken; there is no possibility at this point of undertaking easily repeatable actions. One could regard this conversational process as analogous to dissipative structures arising far from equilibrium. I suggest that when participants cannot hold the anxiety generated at critical levels of mis/understanding, they will abandon the struggle for new meaning and collapse back into previously shared meanings, into words already spoken, or they will engage in increasingly meaningless interaction. Both responses, of course, put an end to the innovation process. However, when relationships are strong enough, the conversational process has the potential for the emergence of new meaning.

Another common pattern in the innovation stories I have told is that when people engage in the kind of conversation that produces emergent new meaning, there is no one who is able to control the flow and direction of the conversation or the meanings that emerge. Even if someone starts a conversation with the intention of suggesting some new idea, the concept will become a temporary stabilization of meaning only after a long period of conversation and it is very likely that the meaning that eventually emerges will be very different from the idea around which the conversation began. Only after this period of conversation will a coherent new pattern of talk emerge, eventually enabling some concrete and tentative action. The emergence of a new pattern of talk implies the first transformation of redundant diversity since it entails the creation/ discovery of an end to pursue. I use the notion of "transformation of redundant diversity" to describe the process by which misunderstanding is reduced so as to enable enough agreement on the meaning of words, sufficient new meaning, to form the basis of the next action. I am talking about temporary stabilizations in mis/understanding in the flow of conversations and I understand conversations to be the essential process of innovation.

To be able to participate in the kind of conversations I am talking about, one must be able to speak within those different patterns of talk that are accepted by other participants. The self-organizing nature of these conversations is constrained by the previous words people have already spoken. This is what keeps the conversation far from equilibrium in bounded instability rather than total randomness. If this were not so, participants would simply give up conversing, because they would not be able to endure the confusion. Or they would collapse redundant diversity, with its potential for misunderstanding, into an already stabilized, repetitive pattern of talk in order to avoid anxiety. Or the conversation would become so full of redundant diversity that no new pattern of talk could emerge; the level of misunderstanding would simply lead to meaningless conversation. The critical aspect of this complex responsive process, therefore, is the joint capacity of participants in a conversation to hold that level of redundant diversity/difference in patterns of talk/ potential for misunderstanding which is critical to the emergence of new patterns of talk and the new meaning embedded in them.

To participate in the kind of conversation I am talking about, one has to take part in a practice, since the pattern of talk is the pattern of action one is able to perform. It is within the practice that people are able to generate the potential for misunderstanding. Without prior experience within some practice, which amounts to a common experience of being together, one does not understand at all and this is very different from the kind of misunderstanding I am talking about. Without prior experience in a given practice one is able to use words to convey meanings that are very general. However, one is not able to speak words having shared understanding of a tacit or narrative nature since that comes only with experience in the community of practice. Paradoxically, this means that one is not able to tap into the potential for misunderstanding in the talk of that community of practice, because that potential depends upon the coherent whole formed by the tacit and explicit knowledge forming the pattern of talk within a practice. I suggest that if Guillermo and Oliveira found themselves in different settings where other patterns of talk formed the basis of operating, that is, formed the experience of being together, they would not "automatically" be able to think differently and so join discussions with the potential for misunderstanding. It would have required some time for them to join in the ongoing relational processes and be included. They would have needed to access the ideological and rhetorical dimensions of the ongoing communication processes. Only then would they have been able to start participating in the conversations.

However, the fact that they showed the ability to engage in the kind of stressful conversations characterized by redundant diversity does not imply that they always would participate in any process of innovation. From the complex responsive process perspective, previous behaviour is not a predictor of future behaviour. Simply because a person has taken part in one innovation process does not necessarily mean that they will take part in another. This is because we cannot assign an innovation to a person or a group because innovation emerges in interaction between persons. Moreover, the innovations identified with Guillermo and Oliveira took a lifetime of experience in engaging in different patterns of talk. Therefore, their single innovation emerges from a trajectory of a life. In addition, these "innovators" not only participated in the formation of "their" innovation but were also formed by it. Their behaviour eventually became rather repetitive and anchored as they reduced the words they were speaking to stable patterns of talk, to words spoken (Shotter, 1993). Actually, afterward, they often refused to accept any criticism of "their" innovations as though their own identity was merged with the innovations they merely helped to create.

Another important common pattern in my conversations with the "innovators" was that those who engaged in the conversations from which innovations emerged were not located within a single organization. This is consistent with the view that patterns of talk must reach critical levels of diversity in order for the potential for new meaning to emerge. However, it appears that these different patterns of talk also constitute the constraint of self-organizing processes of conversation in the sense that it is these patterns, not just any patterns, that organize and are organized by the conversations. There are some criteria, conscious and unconscious, that participants use to rule out some talk while accepting others. These criteria have to do with the degree of proximity of the patterns of talk. There must be a minimal threshold level of previous common meanings in order to avoid complete confusion. This threshold level relates to a common path these patterns of talk have been following. Their search for words already spoken is made primarily within those that were already spoken by them, or by those with whom they feel the proximity. However, this search is not made through any formal procedure. It is made between people who know each other through previous conversations.

Relationship as the condition for living with anxiety

Admission into a relational process does not simply lie in verbal communication but in the unconscious bodily resonance between persons, in which a feeling of trust and proximity arises. It is these feelings that underlie the choice of partners in scientific and commercial projects. People explain their choices by saying, "we chose this partner, because he/she is OK!" or "we got along just fine last time". It is almost always a person rather than an institution that people refer to. However, these aspects of relationship are completely "hidden" in formal reports, particularly those delivered to scientific and economic authorities, when partnerships are explained on the basis of detailed reasons that do not present the whole picture.

For example, during our conversations together, patterns of relationships emerged between me and those involved in the three innovation experiences discussed in this book. They tried to "convert" me into a believer in the innovations they were pursuing and my sustained interest in what they were doing. In all three cases, those involved in the innovation felt that others did not recognize the worth of what they were doing: the superiority (technical, logical, rational, and financial) of their innovation was only "self-evident" to the persons who were promoting it. They went to the trouble of giving me lectures on the technicalities of their field so that I could share in their patterns of talk and so understand what they were doing. Attempts were made to gain my sympathy: several sentences would begin with "we", including me in some positive group affiliation. My interest was sometimes experienced as supportive, a basis of trust. At other times my attempts to remain neutral led to exasperation with what they might have taken as my indifference. I was given the chance to get involved with them because they came to feel that I was a trusted participant. It became clear to me that my efforts to remain "neutral", to retain the position of the detached observer, were counterproductive. The fact that I became emotionally involved, that I liked the innovators and felt biased toward what they were doing was precisely why they involved me.

As they relate to each other in such conversations, people glimpse the project they are trying to realize. They co-opt each other into legitimating what they are doing. Experiences of this kind are often referred to as trust.

People in the innovation experiences recounted in this book acquired trust in their participation in previous conversations from which new streams of talk emerged, or because they simply enjoyed the experience of being together. They sought out those they had previously encountered when they wished to talk about their work. Trust becomes, therefore, a powerful reinforcement of the networks of conversations, as much as the conversations become a reinforcement of trust among the participants. It enables other people to get into conversation characterized by high levels of mis/understanding. Difficulties may arise within the familiar patterns of talk that people feel comfortable with and they may find that they cannot deal with them. Trust then becomes a crucial factor in admitting another into the conversation, one who might bring a new pattern of talk and so help deal with the difficulty.

The emergence of meaning

When some new meaning is developed and accepted, as an organizing theme for a new pattern of talk in the living present, people start to act in a more sequential manner. This is the point that is normally pointed to in mainstream literature as the identification of a need to address and of a product concept to satisfy such a need. This is usually taken as the starting point of the innovation process. However, as I have argued, innovation does not start with a match between a rationally identified need and a set of competencies and tools, purposefully brought together in order to develop a solution. Rather, new meaning arises in ongoing conversations and it will be continually transformed until it is introduced into other conversational processes, namely those of their potential "users", only to be further and further transformed as people in different contexts use the innovation as a tool in their communicative interaction. I suggest that identification of the need is a consequence of success, rather than a precondition for it. The definition of any of the innovations studied was subject to constant and never-ending redefinition. The redefinition of the meaning keeps going even after the innovation is adopted. Indeed, as Slaughter (1993) and Lewis and Seilbold (1993) have pointed out, users tend to recreate the innovation. Rosenberg (1982) points out that after the innovation is concluded, learning occurs when the users actually manipulate it. That is when the innovation becomes a tool of concrete action. This might feed back into the organization where it was developed or it might lead to new transformations in different groups. The need appears to be conceptualized by the users in their use of the innovation, rather than being identified beforehand.

When those who have participated in its creation regard an innovation as "ready", the new meaning is passed on, as an artefact embodying this new knowledge, to a new context. In mainstream literature, this phase is usually described as the launching, or the adoption, of the innovation. The view is that there is either a need to position the innovation in order to attain the previously defined "match", or a need to persuade the potential customers about the superiority of the innovation. In any case, whether a purely rational and programmed process or a more negotiated, idiosyncratic process, both positions posit a unidirectional activity that the promoters seem to control – potential users simply being those whose objections must be overcome.

What my conversations about innovation experience indicate is very different. The adoption phase is similar to the previous conversational phases since now, the new meaning, materialized into some tangible thing, is just the input to new conversational activities where it will act as the enhancer of the potential for misunderstanding. Those exposed to the material outcome of the innovation process will engage in the same kind of redundant conversations as those who created the innovation did before. As far as the potential "adopters" of an innovation are concerned, this potential new meaning simply represents a disruption of their living present, a redundancy in relation to what they were doing. They will appreciate the innovation using their own patterns of talk, not the pattern that emerged among the creators of the innovation. This explains why in the stories in this book, the promoters were sometimes puzzled by the objections made by potential users. The problem was that, although both creators and adapters used the same words to talk about the innovation, they gave the words different meanings.

What emerges out of these conversations between promoters and users is again the reconfiguration of meaning and even of the material and tangible characteristics of the innovation. That is, instead of a simple adoption of "what was there to adopt", the potential users, by conversing with the promoters, force them back again into a period of redundant conversations from which a new understanding will emerge, if the innovation is to be adopted. What might also happen is that the potential users simply refuse to engage in such conversation and, thus, either ignore the new meaning or do not introduce it into their pattern of talk. Or, they might even perceive the new meaning as a direct threat to the words they speak and the words they act upon.

Another important conclusion has to do with the role of power, regardless of its source or legitimacy. If new meaning is taken as a threat, then those among the potential users that are powerful can hinder the conversations, in the same way as powerful people inside an organization can hinder or even stop the flow of redundant conversations required for the discovery of new meanings. In all the innovation experiences, to different degrees, this issue emerged. Powerful players can simply damp the potential for misunderstanding by ruling the new concept out of the legitimate pattern of talking and by making it difficult for others to keep conversing about it.

The institutionalization of meaning

Organizational patterns of talk accommodate the new meaning of an innovation and through enacting it, it becomes part of legitimate speech. It becomes words already spoken. This implies that afterwards there is only one "correct" meaning for the words designating the innovation. Moreover, eventually the new meaning becomes indisputable "fact". However, after this period of assimilation of new meaning, the accepted and legitimate organizational pattern of talk produces another important transformation in the new meaning. Not only does the new meaning become a "fact", implying no possible misunderstanding potential, but also the manner in which that meaning can be deployed is subject to regulation.

This process of convergence from redundancy and misunderstanding to "facts" leads to convergence to a more routine and automatic behaviour based on canonical practices (propositional knowledge). The implications of these transformations are that at an organizational level, relationships gradually move from the trust-based, informal and personal, to the more formal, institutionalized relationships based on economic advantage. The focus on relationships is then on increased efficiency of acting upon words already spoken that carry little misunderstanding potential. However, if one looks only at the final state, one might be tempted to conclude that there is an irrefutable economic advantage in reducing every new meaning to procedures and to formal organizational arrangements as rapidly as possible. One might, therefore, conclude that these processes can be purposefully submitted to some form of social engineering process, making them controllable and manageable. This, I argue, is a crucial mistake, as the new meaning reduced to some words in a manual of operations becomes simply that, some words in a booklet. It will become knowledge only when people develop concrete actions within a complex responsive process, which comprises all levels of symbolic interaction, not just the use of reified symbols.

The challenge to the institutionalization of meaning

The main argument of this book is that formal–conscious–legitimate patterns of communication in organizations create the order and security that people seek. These patterns of meaning in conversation create a social world of identities that is stable enough to enable people to act efficiently. However, at the same time, people in organizations find themselves engaged in disorderly processes of conversation characterized by critical levels of redundant diversity experienced as misunderstanding. In their conversations they seek to transform this misunderstanding into new patterns of meaning. This process might lead to the discovery of new meanings that are, then, enacted in order to yield new patterns of stable identities. In other words, formal–conscious–legitimate patterns of communication are frequently transforming in interaction with informal–conscious/unconscious–shadow conversational themes. Any stabilization soon gives rise to further misunderstanding that people will again find themselves transforming into a meaningful basis for action.

An organization is patterns of meaningful relationships emerging in the tension between the conflicting legitimate and shadow aspects of complex responsive process. The legitimate aspect consists of the official patterns of talk, primarily reflecting widely accepted rules of behaviour. The origin of innovation lies in the shadow aspects of communicative interaction, that is, those themes that are not widely accepted. However, this dialectical process does not guarantee that some beneficial new meaning will replace the old. People may continue in confusion or they may remain locked into old ways of interacting. If the process was a simple linear one, if the shadow facets of the interactions could "automatically" regenerate legitimate patterns, then it would only be a question of "designing" supportive conditions. The innovation experiences recounted in this book point to the essential nonlinearity and interweaving of processes of communicative interaction in which there is no guarantee of success. It is this that makes it impossible to design the process and automatically secure a favourable outcome.

Finally, there is the question of how manageable the processes of innovation are. I suggest that the importance of redundant diversity experienced as misunderstanding makes it clear that conversational activity in any organization cannot be engineered. This means that innovation cannot be managed. The major implication of this book is that we are all participants in communicative interactions having the potential for transformation, that is, innovation. As soon we try to control interaction from an external standpoint, we simply terminate their transformational potential. Instead of elevating the individual as solitary hero of innovation, we come to the more humble realization that it is the quality of participation in ordinary conversation that is the key to innovation.

Bibliography

Abernathy, W.J. and Utterback, J.M. (1988) "Patterns of Industrial Innovation", in Tushman, M.L. and Moore, W.L. (eds) *Readings in the Management of Innovation*, 2nd edn, New York: Harper Row: 55–78.

Ansoff, H.I. and McDonnell, E. (1990) *Implanting Strategic Management*, 2nd edn, Hemel Hempstead: Prentice Hall.

Arthur, W.B. (1996) "Increasing Returns and the New World of Business", *Harvard Business Review*, July–August: 100–108.

Burns, T. and Stalker, G.M. (1961) *Managing Innovation*, London: Tavistock.

Caraça, J.M. (1993) *Do Saber ao Fazer: porquê organizar a ciência*, Lisbon: Gradiva.

Cooper, R.G. (1990) "Stage-gate Systems: a new tool for managing new products", *Business Horizons*, May–June: 44–54.

Cooper, R.G. and Kleinschmidt, E.J. (1991) "New Products: what separates winners from losers?", in Henry, J. and Walker, D. (eds) *Managing Innovation*, London: Sage Publications: 127–140.

Crawford, C.M. (1991) *New Products Management*, 3rd edn, Boston: Irwin.

de Woot, P. (1990) *High Technology Europe: strategic issues for global competition*, Oxford: Basil Blackwell.

Denison, E. (1962) *The Sources of Economic Growth in the United States and the Alternatives Before Us*, London: Allen & Unwin.

Drucker, P.F. (1985) "The Discipline of Innovation", *Harvard Business Review*, May–June: 67–72.

Dussage, P., Harst, S. and Ramanantsoa, B. (1992) *Strategic Technology Management*, Chichester: John Wiley.

Eisenhardt, K.M. and Tabrizi, B.N. (1995) "Accelerating Adaptive Processes: product innovation in the global computer industry", *Administrative Science Quarterly*, 40: 84–110.

Elias, N. (1970) *What is Sociology?* New York: Columbia University Press.

—— (1989) *The Symbol Theory*, London: Sage Publications.

—— (2000) *The Civilizing Process*, Oxford: Basil Blackwell (first published 1939).

Elias, N. and Scotson, J. (1994) *The Established and the Outsiders*, London: Sage Publications.

European Commission (1996) Green paper on Innovation, Brussels: EU.

Freeman, C. (1974) *The Economics of Industrial Innovation*, London: Pinter.

—— (1988) "Introduction", in Dosi, G., Freeman, C., Nelson, R., Silverberg, G. and Soete, L. (eds) *Technical Change and Economic Theory*, London: Pinter: 1–8.

Frost, P.J. and Egri, C.P. (1991) "The Political Process of Innovation", *Research in Organizational Behaviour*, 13: 229–295.

Gibbons, M. and Johnston, R. (1974) "The Role of Science in Technological Innovation", *Research Policy*, 3, 3: 220–242.

Gomory, R.E. (1989) "From the 'Ladder of Science' to the Product Development Cycle", *Harvard Business Review*, Nov.–Dec.: 99–105.

Gould, S.J. (1988) "The Panda's Thumb in Technology", in Tushman, M. and Moore, W. (eds) *Readings in the Management of Innovation*, 2nd edn, New York: Harper Business: 37–44.

Griffin, D. (1998) 'Dealing with the Paradox of Culture in Management Theory', unpublished PhD Thesis, University of Hertfordshire.

—— (2001) *The Emergence of Leadership*, London: Routledge.

Gupta, A. and Wilemon, D. (1990) "Accelerating the Development of Technologically Based New Products", *California Management Review*: 24–44.

Hamel, G. and Prahalad, C.K. (1989) "Strategic Intent", *Harvard Business Review*, May–June: 63–76.

Hannan, M.T. and Freeman, J. (1977) "The Population Ecology of Organizations", *American Journal of Sociology*, 82: 929–964.

Henderson, R. and Clark, K. (1990) "Architectural Innovation: the reconfiguration of existing product technologies and the failure of established firms", *Administrative Science Quarterly*, 35: 9–30.

Howell, J. and Higgins, C. (1990) "Champions of Technological Innovation", *Administrative Science Quarterly*, 35: 317–341.

Johne, A. and Snelson, P. (1990) *Successful Product Innovation*, Oxford: Basil Blackwell.

Kanter, R.M. (1984) *The Change Masters: Corporate Entrepreneurs at Work*, London: Routledge.

—— (1988) "When a Thousand Flowers Bloom: structural, collective, and social conditions for innovation in organization", *Research in Organizational Behavior*, 10: 169–211.

—— (1989) *When Giants Learn to Dance*, London: Routledge.

Kauffman, S. (1995) *At Home in the Universe: the search for laws of complexity*, London: Viking.

Kirton, M. (1980) "Adaptors and Innovators in Organisations", *Human Relations*, 3, 4: 213–224.

Koontz, H., O'Donnell, C. and Weinrich, H. (1984) *Management*, 8th edn, Singapore: McGraw-Hill.

Kotler, P. (1988) *Marketing Management: analysis, planning, implementation and control*, 6th edn, Englewood Cliffs, NJ: Prentice Hall.

Lewis, I.K. and Seilbold, D.R. (1993) "Innovation Modification during Intraorganizational Adoption", *Academy of Management Journal*, 18, 2: 322–354.

Lundvall, B.-A. (1992) "Introduction to National Systems of Innovation", in Lundvall, B.-A. (ed.) *National Systems of Innovation*, London: Pinter: 1–22.

Maidique, M.A. (1988) "Entrepreneurs, Champions, and Technological Development", in Tushman, M.L. and Moore, W.L. (eds) *Readings in the Management of Innovation*, 2nd edn, New York: Harper Business: 565–584.

Marquis, D.G. (1988) "The Anatomy of Successful Innovations", in Tushman, M.L. and Moore, W.L. (eds) *Readings in the Management of Innovation*, 2nd edn, New York: Harper Business: 79–87.

Mead, G.H. (1934) *Mind, Self and Society*, Chicago: Chicago University Press.

Mintzberg, H. (1991) "The Innovative Organization", in Mintzberg, H. and Quinn, J.B. (eds), *The Strategy Process: concepts, contexts, cases*, 2nd edn, Englewood Cliffs, NJ: Prentice Hall: 731–745.

Nelson, R. and Winter, S. (1982) *An Evolutionary Theory of Economic Change*, Cambridge, MA: Harvard University Press.

Nicolis, G. (1989) "Physics of Far-from-equilibrium Systems and Self-organisation", in Davies, P. (ed.) *The New Physics*, Cambridge: Cambridge University Press: 317–347.

Nicolis, G. and Prigogine, I. (1989) *Exploring Complexity: an introduction*, New York: W.H. Freeman.

Pavitt, K. (1984) "Patterns of Technical Change: towards a taxonomy and a theory", *Research Policy*, 13.

Peters, T. and Waterman, R.H. (1982) *In Search of Excellence*, New York: John Wiley.

Porter, M. (1980) *Competitive Strategy: techniques for analysing industries and competitors*, New York: Free Press.

Prigogine, I. (1996) *O Fim das Certezas*, Lisbon: Gradiva.

—— (1998) *The End of Certainty*, Lisbon: Conference in the Gulbenkian Foundation.

Prigogine, I. and Stengers, I. (1984) *Order out of Chaos: man's new dialogue with nature*, New York: Bantam Books.

Quinn, J.B. (1991) "Managing Innovation: controlled chaos", in Mintzberg, H. and Quinn, J.B. (eds) *The Strategy Process: concepts, contexts, cases*, 2nd edn, Englewood Cliffs, NJ: Prentice Hall: 746–758.

Rogers, E.M. (1983) *Diffusion of Innovations*, 3rd edn, New York: Free Press.

Rosenberg, N. (1982) *Inside the Black Box: technology and economics*, Cambridge: Cambridge University Press.

Schein, E. (1988) *Organizational Psychology*, Englewood Cliffs, NJ: Prentice-Hall.

Schumpeter, J.A. (1934) *The Theory of Economic Development: an inquiry into profits, capital, credit, interest, and the business cycles*, Boston: Harvard University Press.

—— (1939) *Business Cycles: a theoretical, historical and statistical analysis of the capitalist process*, 2 vols, New York: McGraw-Hill.

Shotter, J. (1993) *Conversational Realities: constructing life through language*, London: Sage Publications.

Slaughter, S. (1993) "Innovation and Learning during Implementation: a comparison of user and manufacturer innovations", *Research Policy*, 22: 81–95.

Solow, R. (1957) "Technical Change and the Aggregate Production Function", *Review of Economic and Statistics*, 39: 312–320.

Souder, W.E. (1987) *Managing New Product Innovations*, Lexington, MA: Lexington Books.

Stacey, R.D. (2000) *Strategic Management and Organisational Dynamics*, 3rd edn, London: Financial Times-Prentice Hall.

—— (2001) *Complex Responsive Processes in Organizations*, London: Routledge.

Stacey, R.D., Griffin, D. and Shaw, P. (2000) *Complexity and Management: fad or radical challenge to systems thinking*, London: Routledge.

Twiss, B. (1992) *Managing Technological Innovation*, 4th edn, London: Pitman.

Van de Ven, A.H. (1988) "Central Problems in the Management of Innovation", in Tushman, M.L. and Moore, W.L. (eds) *Readings in the Management of Innovation*, 2nd edn, New York: Harper Business: 103–122.

von Hippel, E. (1988) *The Sources of Innovation*, Oxford: Oxford University Press.

Watzlawick, P., Bavelas, J. and Jackson, D. (1967) *The Pragmatics of Human Communication*, New York: W.W. Norton.

Weick, K. (1995) *Sensemaking in Organizations*, London: Sage Publications.

Wheelwright, S.C. and Clark, K.B. (1992) *Revolutionizing Product Development: quantum leaps in speed, efficiency and quality*, New York: Free Press.

Wolfe, R.A. (1994) "Organizational Innovation: review, critique and suggested research directions", *Journal of Management Studies*, 31, 3: 405–431.

Zirger, B. and Maidique, M. (1990) "A Model of New Product Development: an empirical test", *Management Science*, 36: 867–883.

Index

Abernathy, W.J. 2
adopters of innovation 117–18
agent-based modelling 84
Amdahl 99, 102
Ansoff, H.I. 2
anxiety coping, relational processes
    115–16
Arthur, W.B. 6
autonomy of individuals 20, 75
Azevedo, Luis 35

banking, Portugal 37
bar coding 99
Barrera, Guillermo 95; conversation 104;
    EDI 102; experience 96, 97–8;
    experiments 101; informal networking
    102; multinationals 110; see also
    electronic catalogue
behaviour: see human behaviour
bifurcation point: communication 86;
    dissipative structures 82, 87
Brazil 102, 105
Burns, T. 2
bus stop shelters 38, 41

cable maintenance 49
Campos, Carlos 95, 98, 104
Caraça, Bento de Jesus v
Caraça, J.M. 6, 54
catalogue: see electronic catalogue
CEP: Brazilian interests 102, 105;
    collaboration 95, 98, 99; competitors
    109; general manager 108;
    information processing 109–10;

knowledge investors 99, 101, 103,
    107, 108; origins 99; price
    information 109; suppliers 107–8
change 5–6; dissipative structures 82–3;
    identity 78; nonlinearity 6;
    organizations 8; patterns 82–3;
    threatening 48
chaos theory 95
civil construction industry 42
Clark, K. 24
Clark, K.B. 2
collaboration 95, 98, 99
communication: bifurcation points 86;
    complex responsive processes 79, 90;
    emotion 104, 116; innovation 50, 91,
    111–12; meaning 6; misunderstanding
    86, 104–5; nonlinearity 120;
    organizations 76, 96–7, 119–20;
    power relations 104; redundant
    diversity 86–7; relationships 7;
    symbolic 73; water utility 57; see also
    interaction
competition 1, 2; CEP 109;
    entrepreneurship 21; novelty 4; rules
    21
complex responsive processes 70;
    communication 79, 90; human action
    72–4; innovation 5, 8, 50, 71, 74;
    interaction 71–2; organizations 7, 76,
    111; symbolic interaction 119
complexity: doctoral group 51, 52;
    human realities 51, 84; language 53;
    order 51; organizations 51;
    understanding 52

complexity science 8, 70–1
computer scientists, conversation 64
computer simulation 71
concrete manufacturers 36–7
concrete pipes: earthquakes 36; erosion 32; innovation 76–7; longitudinal joints 34; oval sections 33–4; rational planning approach 36; rubber joints 32–3
conformity 30, 31
consumer goods distribution 95–6
consumers 4
control: conformity 30; interaction 75
convection example, dissipative structures 81–2
conversations: Barrera 104; Campos 104; computer scientists 64; dissipative structures 81–5, 88, 111–15; diversity 52–3; doctoral group 52–3; dynamics 93; electronic catalogue 104; engineers 62, 64; informal/formal 50, 54–5; innovation 69–70, 114–15, 120; interaction 57, 73; interdisciplinary 62; knowledge 112–13; Oliveira 44–5, 47–9, 76–7, 79; patterns 91–2, 114, 115; self-organization 113; shadow themes 89–90; stress 114; transformation 8–9; trust 50
Cooper, R.G. 2, 18, 28
corporate culture 22
craftsmanship 56
Crawford, C.M. 1, 2, 18, 19, 28
creative destruction 21
culture: corporate 22; craftsmanship 56; differences 52; entrepreneurial/social approach 56; leadership 22, 26; organizations 77, 80–1; politics 22–5; vision 27
cybernetic systems 27

Darwin, C. 15
de Woot, P. 2
decision-making 55–6
Denison, E. 13
difference 52–3, 79
digitized survey, water utility 54–5, 59–61, 78, 79–80;

entrepreneurial/social approach 66; evolving 64–7; interaction 77; misunderstanding 87–8; power relations 78; as process control system 65; rational planning approach 66; revision 61–2; testing 62–3; training courses 63–4
dissipative structures 8; bifurcation point 82, 87; change patterns 82–3; convection example 81–2; conversation 81–5, 88, 111–15; economics 84; interaction 85–7; meaning 88–9; nature 84; novelty 83; organizations 88, 92–3; redundant diversity 86
Distribuição Hoje 97, 99
doctoral group: complexity 51, 52; conversations 52–3; misunderstanding 53–4
Drucker, P.F. 18
duplication, organizations 59
Dussage, P. 2
dynamics: conversation 93; human behaviour 85; interaction 71; see also power relations

EAN 99, 102
earthquakes 36
economics 2; classical 11–12; dissipative structures 84; evolutionary 3, 11, 14–17, 30; mathematical models of growth 13; neoclassical 12–14, 15
EDI (Electronic Data Interchange): image transmissions 102; ISOCOR 103; protocols 101–2; standards 97, 106
Egri, C.P. 2, 22–3
Eisenhardt, K.M. 1
electronic catalogue 97, 100–3, 106–10; alliance of companies 98; benefits 105–6; conversation 104; currency 99, 102; data collection of sales 100; data-warehouse 100; EDI 97, 101–2, 103, 106; encryption programme 103, 106; EU 98, 99, 109; information 99–100; Internet 103, 105, 106; language 99, 102, 104; local businesses 96, 107–8; multimedia

100; ordering/invoicing/paying 100;
political implications 107, 110; price
differentiation 108–9; product
information sheet 101–2; product
verification 103; protocols 98;
redundant diversity 106; security of
information 109; software solutions
106; text 100; understanding 104; *see
also* Barrera, Guillermo
Electronic Data Interchange: *see* EDI
Elias, Norbert 73
emotion, communication 104, 116
empowerment, leadership theory 23
encryption programme 103, 106
Engil 38, 41
engineers, conversation 62, 64
entrepreneurial/social approach: culture
56; digitized survey 66; innovation
30–1
entrepreneurship: competition 21;
individuals 24, 26; Kanter 24;
leadership 30; Oliveira 40–1, 43,
44–7; Schumpeter 14, 15–16
entropy 86
environment for innovation 23, 25–6
Epal: background 55–6; decision-making
55–6; digitized survey 54–5, 59–61,
66–7; information flows 58;
innovation 112
EU: electronic catalogue 109; European
Act (1986) 1
Eurociber 99
European Act (1986) 1
evolutionary economics 3, 11, 14–17, 30
evolutionary theory 15
expectations, organizations 89

Fernandes, Valadas 35
Figueira da Foz sea wall 39, 41
Freeman, C. 2, 6
Freeman, J. 21
Frost, P.J. 2, 22–3

Gama, Vasco da 5
General Electric 97
Gibbons, M. 2
globalization 5–6
Gomory, R.E. 2

Gonçalves, Fernando 31
Gould, S.J. 2
Griffin, D. 26, 71, 80
Gupta, A. 28
Gupta Technologies 99

Hamel, G. 24
Hannan, M.T. 21
Henderson, R. 24
Hidrotécnica 39
Higgins, C. 2, 24
high technology industries 2
Howell, J. 2, 24
human agents: complex responsive
processes 72–4; innovation 2–3;
organizations 75–6
human behaviour: complexity 51, 84;
determinants 16–17; dynamics 85;
systemic approach 64

IBM 99, 107
identity: change 78; evolving 8;
interaction 8, 80; local 96; Oliveira
46–7; transformation 110
individuals: autonomy 20, 75;
entrepreneurship 24, 26; innovation
29, 69; leadership theory 24;
organizations 7; rational 12; social
system 70
information 96; electronic catalogue
99–100; Epal 58; revolution 6
information databases, retail industry
97
information processing 109–10
Informix 99
innovation 66–7, 80–1; communication
50, 91, 111–12; complex responsive
processes 5, 8, 50, 71, 74;
conversation 69–70, 114–15, 120;
individuals 29, 69; interaction 71;
Kanter 1, 2, 3, 23–4, 25, 26, 28, 43;
organizations 1, 2, 16–17, 18, 24;
politics 22–3; power relations 42–3,
65, 67–8, 78–9, 106, 110; resistance to
23; revolutionary systems 67–8;
Schumpeter 14–15; transformation
8–9; trust 115–16
instability 24

interaction: complex responsive processes 71–2; control 75; conversation 57, 73; digitized survey 77; dissipative structures 85–7; dynamics 71; identity 8, 80; innovation 5, 8, 50, 71, 74; natural sciences 70–1; nonlinearity 74; organizations 56, 89; self-organization 73; symbolic 73, 119; understanding 86; *see also* communication
interdisciplinarity 52, 62, 93–4
Internet 103, 105, 106
ISOCOR encryption programme 103

Johne, A. 2, 28
Johnston, R. 2

Kanter, R.M.: entrepreneur 24; innovation 1, 2, 3, 23–4, 25, 26, 28, 43; mysticism 27; politics 22; teamwork 24
Kauffman, S. 84
Kirton, M. 2, 24, 44
Kleinschmidt, E.J. 2, 28
knowledge 14–15; conversation 112–13; meaning 8, 112; organizations 80; reified 9
knowledge investors 99, 101, 103, 107, 108
Koontz, H. 19
Kotler, P. 2, 16

language: complexity 53; electronic catalogue 99, 104; misunderstanding 52, 95
law, natural/economic 12
leadership theory 22, 23, 24, 26, 30
Lewis, I.K. 117
Lisbon University 38–9, 41
local businesses 96, 107–8
logistics, retail industry 96
loosely coupled systems 86
Lotus Notes 107
Lundvall, B.-A. 2

McDonnell, E. 2
Maidique, M.A. 2, 28
management theory 11, 16

marketing 2, 16
Marquis, D.G. 2
mathematical models of growth 13
Mead, George Herbert 72
meaning: communication 6; dissipative structures 88–9; emerging 116–18; institutionalization 118–19; knowledge 8, 112; misunderstanding 87; organizations 118–19; reconfigured 118; stabilized 91, 113, 119; transformation 103–6, 107, 119–20
Microsoft 99
Mintzberg, H. 2
mistakes 67
misunderstanding: communication 86, 104–5; digitized survey 87–8; doctoral group 53–4; language 52, 95; meaning 87; redundant diversity 53–4, 86–7, 106; removal of 29–30, 53–4; transformed 113–14, 119
Mobel 34–5, 38–9, 41, 48
multinationals 99, 110
mysticism 27

NASA, Phased Project Planning 18–19
National Laboratory of Civil Engineering 35–6
nature, dissipative structures 84
Nelson, R. 22
networks, informal 36, 40, 47, 102
Nicolis, G. 81, 84–5
Nielsen 99, 109
nonlinearity: change 6; communication 120; innovation 94; interaction 74
novelty 75–6; competition 4; difference 79; dissipative structures 83; innovation 4–5, 26; instability 24

Oliveira, Martins de: awards 37, 40; bus stop shelters 38, 41; career 31, 32–3; concrete pipe design 32–6, 38; conversations 44–5, 47–9, 76–7, 79; entrepreneurship 40–1, 43, 44–7; identity 46–7; innovation 33, 34–6, 44–6, 76–7; Mobel 34–5; networks 36, 40; officialdom 47; patented products 38, 41; personal life 44, 46;

politics 36; power relations 78; questioning approach 44; rational planning approach 36, 40–1, 43; sea erosion 39–40; setbacks 41–3; technical gallery 31, 38–9, 41, 49; venture capital 37–8
Oracle 99
order/complexity 51
organizations: change 8; communication 76, 96–7, 119–20; complex responsive processes 7, 76, 111; complexity 51; culture 77, 80–1; dissipative structures 88, 92–3; duplication 59; expectations 89; human agents 75–6; individuals 7; innovation 1, 2, 16–17, 18, 24; interaction 56, 89; knowledge 80; meaning 118–19; repetitive patterns 77–8; self-referentiality 80; social practice 7–8; transformative patterns 79, 94

paradox of innovation 4–5
Pararede 99, 101, 109
Parsons, Talcott 30
partnerships 115
patterns: change 82–3; conversation 91–2, 114, 115; emergence 84; propagation 85; repetitive 77–8; understanding 86
Pavitt, K. 2
Peters, T. 22
Phased Project Planning, NASA 18–19
Pimenta, Carlos 37
politics: culture 22–5; electronic catalogue 107, 110; innovation 22–3; Oliveira 36
population ecology theory 21
Porter, M. 2
Portugal: banking 37; consumer goods distribution 95–6; electronic catalogue 109; explorations 5; innovation 4; Lisbon University 38–9, 41; see also water utility
Portugal Telecom 99
power relations: communication 104; digitized survey 78; innovation 42–3, 65, 67–8, 78–9, 106, 110; Oliveira 78; see also dynamics

Prahalad, C.K. 24
price differentiation 108–9
Prigogine, I. 8, 81, 82, 84, 85, 86
Procter & Gamble 110
product concept 116–17
product information sheet 101–2
product verification 103
propagation 85

questioning approach 44
Quinn, J.B. 2, 25
Quintela, Professor 32

rational choice theory 5
rational planning approach 28; concrete pipes 36; digitized survey 66; innovation 18–20; Oliveira 36, 40–1, 43
redundancy 85–6, 119
redundant diversity: communication 86–7; dissipative structures 86; electronic catalogue 106; misunderstanding 53–4, 86–7, 106; transformation 113
re-engineering process 65–6
relational processes: anxiety coping 115–16; communication 7; complex responsive process 5, 7; interaction 3–4; see also power relations
repetitive patterns 77–8
research and development 21–2, 91–2
retail industry: information databases 97; locally based 99; logistics 96; relationship with suppliers 105
revolutionary systems 67–8
risk taking 23, 40
Rogers, E.M. 16
Rosenberg, N. 117

Schein, E. 22, 30
Schumpeter, J.A.: creative destruction 21; entrepreneurship 14, 15–16; evolutionary economics 30
science: complexity 70–1; innovation 1–2, 21–2; knowledge 21–2
Scotson, J. 73
screening 19
sea wall, Figueira da Foz 39, 41

Seilbold, D.R. 117
self-improvement 56
self-organization 73, 92, 112, 113
self-referentiality 80
sewage systems 31–3
shadow themes, conversation 89–90
Shaw, P. 71
Shotter, J. 51, 80, 114
SIBS 100, 102, 103, 105, 106
Sintra 31–3
Slaughter, S. 117
Snelson, P. 2, 28
social constructionism 51
social practice, organizations 7–8
social systems 70
software, electronic catalogue 106
Solow, R. 13
Sonae 96, 97
Souder, W.E. 2, 18
spontaneity 27
SSA 99
Stacey, R.D.: adaptionist teleology 15;
    complex responsive processes 7, 70,
    71, 72; formative teleology 15;
    innovation 3; natural law teleology 12;
    novelty 76; shadow themes 89–90
Stalker, G.M. 2
Stengers, I. 8, 81
strategic alliance policy 98
strategic choice theory 21
strategic planning 2
stress/conversation 114
SulPedip 37–8
suppliers 105, 107–8
symbolic interaction 119
symbols, significance 72–3
Synon Inc 99
systemic approach, human behaviour 64
systemic sociology 30
systems thinking 19–20, 76

Tabrizi, B.N. 1
Tagus bridge 41
teamwork 24
technical galleries: cable maintenance
    49; Lisbon University 38–9, 41;
    misunderstanding 87–8; vested
    interests 48–9; world heritage sites 42
technology 3, 13

Telefónica 109
teleology: adaptionist 15, 16, 21, 22, 72;
    formative 15, 16, 20, 22, 72; natural
    law 12, 13, 15, 20, 72; rationalist 12,
    13–14, 15, 16, 18, 20; transformative
    71–2
Telepac 99
thermodynamics 84
training courses, digitized survey 63–4
transformation: conversations 8–9;
    identity 110; innovation 8–9; meaning
    103–6, 107, 119–20;
    misunderstanding 113–14, 119;
    organizations 79, 94; redundant
    diversity 113; teleology 71–2
trust: conversations 50; innovation
    115–16; partnerships 115
Twiss, B. 2

uncertainty 30
understanding 29–30; complexity 52;
    electronic catalogue 104; human
    interaction 86; patterns 86
Unilever 110
United Nations, Electronic Data
    Interchange standards 97
Utterback, J.M. 2

Van de Ven, A.H. 2, 24–5, 44
venture capital 37–8
vested interests, technical galleries 48–9
vision/culture 27
von Hippel, E. 2

water utility 54–5; communication 57;
    departmental organization 55–6;
    digitized survey 54–5, 59–61, 78,
    79–80; duplication 59; repairs to
    distribution system 57–9
Watermann, R.H. 22
Watzlawick, P. 27, 90
Weick, K. 48
Wheelwright, S.C. 2
Wilemon, D. 28
Winter, S. 22
Wolfe, R.A. 2
world heritage sites 42

Zirger, B. 28

Printed in the United States
119156LV00003B/3-4/A